Modern Training and Physiology
for Middle and Long-Distance Runners

John Davis

RunningWritings.com

Copyright © 2013 & 2015 by Running Writings, LLC.
All rights reserved.
ISBN 9780615790299

All copyrighted photos are property of their respective owners
and are used with permission. This book may not be distributed
without permission, either digitally or in print. The information
in this book is not intended as a substitute for medical advice or
treatment, and though the author has made his best effort to as-
sure accuracy, the author and publisher make no guarantee or
claim to absolute completeness or correctness.

Cover photo: Phil Roeder

Contents

Preface

To the reader:

My first serious foray into writing about running was Basic Training Principles for Middle and Long-Distance Running, a short booklet that condensed and simplified the training methods of legendary coach Arthur Lydiard. His training model, which broadly consists of a long period of high-volume aerobic training before more specific anaerobic and race-specific workouts, is the basis for most modern training programs, and as such functions as a very good introduction to the world of training literature for high school and college runners and their coaches. It was meant to be a short, simple, and straightforward booklet that could set a young runner or new coach on the right track towards long-term development.

The feedback I have gotten in response to Basic Training has been overwhelmingly positive, so I felt obliged to synthesize a sequel of sorts—a longer, more detailed guide to some of the nuances of modern training philosophies. If you are completely new to training literature, I suggest you read Basic Training (available for free on my website, RunningWritings.com) before delving into this book, as many of the chapters assume familiarity with some of the terminology outlined in Basic Training.

In addition, there have been significant changes in the running world since the days of "old-school" athletes like Peter Snell, Murray Halberg, and Barry Magee. Many coaches and athletes attempt to use principles like the aerobic and anaerobic thresholds without completely understanding how they work. My intent is to guide you through some of the recent developments in physiology and coaching, hopefully leading you to better training and racing.

This book does not claim to be an exhaustive collection of all possible information on the subjects it covers. Rather, it is a short but rigorous introduction to the practical applications of exercise physiology and modern training techniques, from fundamental workouts to ancillary training and nutrition. This book will be most valuable to the aspiring student of the sport. It should act as a springboard into learning more about the art and science of long-distance running.

One final note: understanding a few of the concepts presented here requires some knowledge of basic chemistry and biology. In particular, the sections on energy pathways and physiological adaptations to training may seem a bit dense if you lack exposure to these subjects. However, with diligence and perhaps some outside research (remember, this book is a springboard!), you should be able to get a solid grasp on these topics. Each chapter also ends with a brief summary which distills the most important information presented in that chapter without getting too technical.

—*John Davis*

May 2013
Revised June 2015

Introduction

The human body has changed very little since Peter Snell thundered to victory in the 800m at the 1960 Summer Olympics, but our understanding of it, and the application of that understanding, have been updated dramatically in the past several decades. The rise of more scientific training, modern lifestyles and habits, and the dominance of the East Africans at the international level have changed the way we look at distance running in the twenty-first century. Hardly fifty years ago, there were only a handful of four-minute milers in the world. Today, the world record is 3:43.13. In addition, the women's marathon world record has dropped by an *hour* since 1967.

How are such drastic advances in running ability possible? Fifty years is not long enough for any significant changes in the genetics of humankind, nor have the improvements been from any one corner of the world. National records have fallen everywhere from America to Ireland to Kenya to Japan. The only explanation for this upward trend is the augmentation of basic training principles established in the '60s and '70s with modern-day advances in physiology and coaching wisdom. Coaches and athletes who have drawn on both have seen huge success, while those who attempt to rely exclusively on "old school" training or modern "scientifically proven" training have been left behind.

This book outlines some of the most important advances in training in the past fifty years. The topics range from fundamental training principles to useful ancillary work—insignificant on its own, but part of a complete training program when combined with the more foundational elements of preparing for middle and long-distance races.

Chapter 1
Energy Pathways

To understand the basics of training for distance races, it is necessary to learn how the body actually generates the fuel it needs to move itself forward while running. While complicated, these mechanisms ultimately determine how far you can run and at what speeds. The fundamental question of training—"How do I improve my race times?"—can only be answered with a training plan that respects the physiology of movement.

In your muscles, all energy is generated by breaking down a molecule called **adenosine triphosphate** (ATP) into adenosine **di**phosphate (ADP), a phosphate ion (P_i), and a proton (H^+):

$$ATP + H_2O \leftrightarrow ADP + P_i + H^+ + \textbf{Energy}$$

Adding water to this phosphate bond releases a great deal of energy, which is used to contract muscle fibers. When we speak of "energy pathways," we are discussing the various ways ATP can be supplied to the muscles. ATP is regenerated by rejoining spent ADP and a free phosphate ion, P_i, which can happen through a variety of processes.

There are four main energy pathways used in high-intensity running, each of which plays an important role in training and racing.

1. Stored ATP

At rest, there is a small amount of stored ATP available in the muscles. When a sprinter bursts out of the blocks in the 200m, she is being fueled by her stored ATP. This energy is depleted in only a few seconds. For exercise to continue, ATP needs to be regenerated by rejoining spent ADP and phosphate ions. The body has several ways to do this.

2. The Phosphocreatine System

When stored ATP is nearly depleted, the phosphocreatine system kicks in, breaking down **phosphocreatine**, a molecule found in the muscles, into creatine and phosphate. The phosphate is donated to the spent ADP, which quickly combines with it to form ATP. The phosphocreatine system works for approximately eight seconds during an all-out effort. So, our 200m sprinter, who depletes her stored ATP after two to four seconds, relies primarily on the phosphocreatine system until roughly ten seconds into the race. Though these energy systems may seem insignificant to a distance runner, it is the stored ATP and the phosphocreatine system that enable you to "get off the line" at the start of a race, as well as launch into a powerful kick at the end. While football players take creatine supplements to gain power by boosting the phosphocreatine system, the weight gain and water retention associated with it offset any possible benefit in runners.

3. The Glycolysis or Anaerobic System

After the phosphocreatine system is depleted, the body needs another way to rapidly reform ATP. Glucose, a simple form of sugar present in abundant quantities in muscle tissue (often in a polymer form called **glycogen**), is the fuel of choice. In a long chain of reactions, enzymes inside muscle cells break down glucose into a smaller compound called **pyruvate**, releasing two protons and regenerating two molecules of ATP from ADP. This process is called **glycolysis**. No oxygen from the blood is required for this reaction, so it is an **an-aerobic** energy system. In order to counteract the protons released when glucose is broken down, the body converts the pyruvate into **lactate**. This process consumes protons, and lactate can also "shuttle" protons out of the muscle cells and release them into the bloodstream, which further reduces localized proton buildup. Eventually, lactate is broken down for energy elsewhere in the body.

Your body has the capacity to produce an enormous amount of energy very quickly using the glycolysis system; the only problem is that the waste products from such high ATP turnover build up over time. While ADP, creatine, and phosphate (waste products from the phosphocreatine system and the breakdown of ATP) can be reused easily and don't build up in large concentrations, the protons released from breaking down large amounts of ATP cause serious problems by increasing the acidity in your muscle cells and your blood.

There are various buffering mechanisms in your body to slow the buildup of acidity in the muscles during high-intensity exercise, but ultimately, these only last about 35-45 seconds in an all-out effort. At this point, the acidity inside the muscle cells severely impairs muscular contraction and extreme fatigue sets in. This condition is called **acidosis**. "Running anaerobically" and "incurring oxygen debt" are often-used terms that mean relying on glycolysis for the bulk of your energy. Our 200m runner relies largely on the glycolysis (or anaerobic) system to get through the last sixteen seconds of her race if she runs her competition in 26 seconds.

In the past, exercise physiologists blamed "lactic acid buildup" for fatigue during high-intensity efforts. If we took a blood sample of our 200m runner immediately after her race, we would find a high concentration of protons and lactate. Only in the last ten years have scientists recognized that, while found together, lactate and protons are produced through different processes in the muscles during exercise.[1] Though lactate does not impair performance, it tracks very well with acid levels in the blood and muscles, so it is nevertheless a good indirect measurement of the amount of acid building up in an athlete's body.

4. The Aerobic System

The most robust way your body can regenerate ATP and reduce proton buildup is with the aerobic system. It becomes an important factor for performance in any event that lasts longer than the anaerobic system's all-out potential—35-45 seconds. While all of the previous energy systems can work anywhere within the muscles, aerobic ATP production can only take place in special structures inside muscle cells called **mitochondria**. Pyruvate, protons, ADP, phosphate, and most importantly **oxygen** from the blood all must be transported into the mitochondria for the aerobic system to function. However, it is incredibly efficient, producing 36-38 ATP molecules per molecule of glucose consumed. The first step in this process—the glycolysis system breaking glucose down into two pyruvate molecules—only yields two of these ATP molecules. Additionally, the only waste products from the aerobic system are water and carbon dioxide, which can be easily disposed of via the blood and lungs. The aerobic system *consumes* protons, reducing the level of acidity in the muscles. When running at slow to moderate speeds, the aerobic system can also burn fat in place of glucose.

The aerobic system is the rate-limiting factor when it comes to sustainably producing energy in a distance race. If the rate of ATP breakdown does not exceed the mitochondria's ability to process pyruvate and protons, levels of lactate and acidity will be stable in the muscles and acidosis will not occur. However, when you exceed the capacity of your aerobic system, the additional energy to maintain the faster pace will come directly from the anaerobic system, causing protons and lactate to build up. In a race such as the 10,000m, you will perhaps be exceeding your aerobic capacity by 10%, so

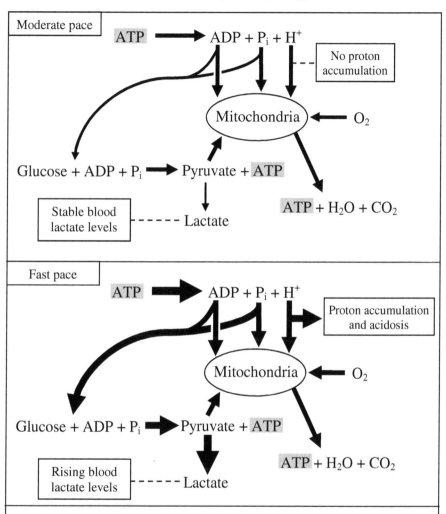

When the mitochondria can keep up with the amount of ATP demanded during exercise, no acid accumulates and blood lactate levels are stable (top). When the energy demands of exercise outstrip the body's capability to replenish ATP aerobically using the mitochondria, the glycolysis system supplies the extra ATP needed, leading to an increase in blood lactate levels. However, because glycolysis does not consume protons when it reforms ATP, the protons released when ATP is broken down accumulate and increase the acidity of the muscle cell (bottom).
Note that the equations in this chart are neither balanced nor chemically complete.

acidity is slowly increasing, but not enough to cause significant strain until 15 or 20 minutes into the race.

Now that you have an understanding of the interplay between the aerobic and anaerobic systems, it is clear why your aerobic fitness plays a fundamental role in your overall running ability: if your mitochondria cannot keep pace with the ATP turnover demanded by your running speed, acidity will build up in your muscles very quickly. In contrast, having a strong aerobic system allows you to maintain a fast pace for a long time without becoming fatigued. To this end, the centerpiece of any long-term training program has to be developing a powerful aerobic system, since improvements in your ability to run quickly *without* generating acidity enable tremendous speed and stamina when you *do* rely on your anaerobic system for additional energy.

Lastly, it is important to note that metabolic fatigue—the result of ATP turnover in excess of your aerobic system's capacity—is not the only type of fatigue. Muscular fatigue can occur when the fibers that make up your muscles become damaged and cannot contract as strongly. Energy depletion is another type of fatigue which happens when your muscles *run out* of glucose to burn for fuel. These types of fatigue are the reason you feel tired after a long, continuous easy run, and are a significant factor in marathon running. Finally, your central nervous system, which controls your muscles, can become fatigued after very taxing efforts like repeated sprints, racing, or doing frequent, hard interval workouts too often.

Chapter 1 Summary

While the various components of the body's energy system appear complicated, understanding their role and function enables a more informed training philosophy. Because protons will *always* be generated when running at moderate to high speeds (due to the inherently high ATP turnover associated with fast paces), you can see why aerobic conditioning should form the foundation of your training. Even though the anaerobic system can put out an incredible amount of energy, it has no way to prevent the buildup of acid in your muscles and your blood. The only way your body *can* do this is through the aerobic system. Strong aerobic fitness allows you to maintain a high rate of ATP synthesis without allowing protons to accumulate.

Chapter 2
Theory into Practice: The Aerobic and Anaerobic Thresholds

Knowledge of energy pathways is only important to you if it can be applied in your training. Fortunately, advances by exercise physiologists, most notably Jack Daniels of Daniels' Running Formula fame, have revealed training methods which can shift the body's use of energy pathways and result in faster race times.

If we take an untrained man and put him on a treadmill at ten-minute-mile pace, he will be exhausted after only a few minutes. However, a well-trained athlete can easily handle such a pace since his body is conditioned to operate aerobically at that speed. If we used a probe to measure his blood lactate level, it would be very low: in the range of 1.0-1.5 mM (mmol/L or millimoles of lactate molecules per liter of blood). If we slowly increased this pace to 9, 8, and 7 minutes per mile, his blood lactate level would not change significantly. He is running aerobically because his mitochondria can produce the bulk of his required energy. His body is not allowing any additional lactate (or protons) to accumulate.

However, as we continue to gradually increase the pace to 6 minutes per mile or faster, his blood lactate would begin to increase at a slow but steady rate. This point is the

aerobic threshold, or **AT**; it is the fastest pace which will not become progressively more difficult to maintain (or, in other words, the slowest pace which exceeds the body's ability to keep lactate and acidity levels stable). This is also sometimes called your "maximum steady state" or "marathon pace," as it corresponds to your theoretical pace in a marathon, discounting muscular fatigue and fueling issues.

If we increase the pace further, our runner's blood lactate level will increase slowly, but he can continue for quite some time. Once his blood lactate level rises to about 4.0 mM, any increase in pace will result in an exponential rise in blood lactate. This is the traditional definition of the **anaerobic** or **lactate threshold**. Both terms are used, often interchangeably, by different sources. For consistency, this book will be using "anaerobic threshold" or **AnT**. An athlete's individual anaerobic threshold may not be exactly 4.0 mM, but its actual value does not need to be known for training purposes. Well-trained athletes can *feel* when they are running at their aerobic and anaerobic thresholds. Developing your ability to sense these paces is very important for improving them.

Soon after the discovery of the aerobic and anaerobic thresholds, physiologists and coaches wondered if specific kinds of training would increase these thresholds so an athlete could run at a given pace with less effort and incur less acid buildup. The answer is **YES**.

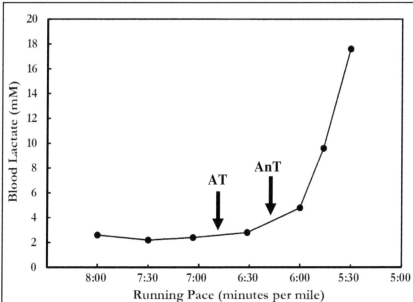

A blood lactate level test with the *approximate* AT and AnT labeled. As running pace increases, blood lactate levels begin to rise exponentially once the body's aerobic system cannot produce enough energy to support the increased pace.

Data courtesy Greg Rhodes, University of Minnesota Human and Sport Performance Laboratory & Owner of Endurance Athlete

Training the Aerobic Threshold

Since it is a direct reflection of your aerobic fitness, training the aerobic threshold is fairly straightforward: time spent running at or below it will result in its increase. So, 60 minutes of jogging will slightly increase the AT, as will 60 minutes at a brisk pace, but faster paces have a greater effect on the AT. Running at or near the aerobic threshold for long durations during the "base," "conditioning," or "aerobic development" phase of a training program (summer and winter for most high school and college runners) will go a long way towards improving your fitness.

Many coaches recommend "**tempo runs**" or **AT runs** of 30-60 minutes at the aerobic threshold once a week during the base phase. An aerobic threshold run should feel fast but relaxed. It should not get progressively more difficult; if it does, you are exceeding your aerobic threshold, which is counterproductive.

Training the Anaerobic Threshold

The anaerobic threshold responds to aerobic training similarly; as you increase your AT, your AnT will increase as well. But to adequately train all aspects of your energy systems, it is helpful to specifically target the anaerobic threshold in training. Scientific research spearheaded by acclaimed American coach and researcher Jack Daniels has confirmed that running at the AnT, either in a sustained run or in long repetitions with short recovery, can increase the anaerobic threshold, leading to faster race times.

Daniels also researched how an athlete's lab-measured aerobic and anaerobic thresholds correspond to his or her personal records over a variety of distances. From his research, he formulated a master table that can provide a good estimate of an athlete's AT and AnT based on his or her recent race times. An abbreviated version of this chart can be found in Appendix A (p. 70).

Running at the Anaerobic Threshold:
AnT Runs and Cruise Intervals

The anaerobic threshold, since it *is*, after all, an anaerobic pace, cannot be sustained for very long periods of time like the aerobic threshold. The AnT is often quoted as a pace that can be maintained in an all-out race lasting 50-60 minutes. Daniels recommends that the total distance of your individual AnT workouts be less than 10% of your weekly mileage.

The Progression Run

In Kenya, one of the staple workouts of runners from novices to Olympic champions is the progression run. It begins at a leisurely jog, but over the next few miles, the pace slowly increases. After 4-5 miles, the pace has progressed to around the aerobic threshold, where it plateaus until only a mile or two remain. In the final portion, the pace increases to the anaerobic threshold and sometimes slightly past it.

Kenyans often do progression runs in large groups, with the last mile being playfully competitive. But they are smart enough to back off when the pace becomes too strenuous. A summer training group I started for up-and-coming high school and college runners used progression runs once a week, with a "one more mile" rule: you must finish feeling as though you could run one more mile ten seconds faster than the last. Of course, we never *actually* ran another mile afterward.

Progression runs are one of the best workouts for learning to run **fast** without running **hard**, as you are increasing the pace continuously, but always holding back a bit. They are also conducive to being done in large groups. Because they start laughably slow, runners with a huge range of abilities can run together, with slower runners simply ending the workout earlier and jogging the rest of the run.

An **anaerobic threshold run** or **AnT run** is a sustained run of 3-4 miles (or 15-25 minutes) at the anaerobic threshold. The pace should be even, neither speeding up significantly nor slowing down much at the end. An AnT run will have a fast, "flying" feeling, and may get uncomfortable in the last mile or so, but should not be extremely fatiguing. Confusingly, these are also sometimes called "tempo runs." It is important to remember that AT runs and AnT runs are very different. An AnT run should not be much longer than 25 minutes, because it will lead to excessive acidosis and counteract the benefits of the workout.

A **cruise interval workout** is a set of long repetitions at the AnT with relatively short recovery. Daniels recommends that the repeats be between 3 and 15 minutes in length (keeping in mind the upper limit of 10% of one's weekly mileage) with approximately one minute of jogging recovery per five minutes of running. Cruise intervals are advantageous because they allow you to spend more total time running at the anaerobic threshold than an AnT run. They are also a fairly versatile workout since they hardly incur any oxygen debt, so they can be done during the base phase as a high-volume workout for aerobic development, during the anaerobic development phase as a medium-duration maintenance session, and during the racing phase as a light, relaxed workout a few days out from a race.

Let's say you're a high school runner who recently ran a 3200m PR of 10:00. If we look up your predicted aerobic and anaerobic thresholds in Appendix A, we find that Daniels' chart predicts an AT of 5:54 per mile and an AnT of 5:36 per mile, or 3:29 per km. If you are running around 50 miles per week, a sensible workout for boosting your aerobic threshold might be a 30-35 minute (5-6mi) AT run at about 5:54 mile pace. A good anaerobic threshold workout might be an AnT run of 20 minutes at 5:36 per mile, or a cruise interval workout consisting of 5 to 7 1000m repeats in 3:29, with 45-60 seconds of jogging recovery between repeats.

Problems with Using a Predictive Formula

Now, suppose you set off diligently on a warm summer afternoon to complete our prescribed workout of 6x1000m in 3:29. You feel sluggish on your warmup and your first repeat is four seconds slow, but, not wanting to shrink from the task, you grimace your face, gut it out, and run the final five repeats in 3:29. You are rather tired by the end. Have you accomplished what you set out to do? This time, the answer is an emphatic **NO**.

Threshold training is also a mental exercise; the AT and AnT are primarily *feelings*, not paces written in stone. Advances in scientific training do not excuse you from listening to your own body. Workouts at the aerobic and anaerobic thresholds should not be exhausting. Sometimes, due to wind, heat, the rigors of training, or simply the mysteries of the body, your TRUE threshold is not what is written in a chart. You must learn what the AT and AnT *feel* like and use your watch only for reference in these workouts. Sixty-one-minute half-marathoner George "Malmo" Malley puts it best: "**I'm trying to get you to 'feel' kung fu, not 'think' it.**" Keep in mind that the right pace today may not be the right one tomorrow, and that your day-to-day variations may not match up with those of your teammates. The key to running threshold workouts (of both types) is learning to run *fast* without running *hard*.

Another problem associated with using formulas and charts is what I call "aerobic drift." Let's return to our example of you as a ten-minute two-miler. Your mile PR will likely be somewhere in the vicinity of 4:37, give or take a bit depending on whether you are better at the middle or long distances. If you ran a 10km road race over the summer, you would be very lucky if you could break 35:00. However, if we consult a performance chart, we find that a 4:37 mile equates to a 9:53 2-mile and an astonishing 33:01 10k. Should you give up all hope on the longer distances? Hardly.

Especially for younger runners, attempts to predict training paces from mile or even two-mile times are often inaccurate because you have only been training for a few years, and your aerobic system is still very underdeveloped. Hence, on a chart of equivalent performances, a line connecting your PRs tends to "drift" towards slower times as the distance increases. So, if we predict your AnT from your mile PR, we will get a different number than if we predict it from your two-mile or 5k PR. Generally, the best approach is to be conservative with predicted paces. Trusting a chart too much will run you into the ground more often than it will hold you back.

Chapter 2 Summary

The aerobic and anaerobic thresholds are useful concepts in training, as they are a direct reflection of the fitness of your aerobic system. Long, continuous runs called AT runs can improve the aerobic threshold, while cruise interval workouts and shorter continuous runs called AnT runs can be used to improve the anaerobic threshold. While pace charts such as the one included in Appendix A (p. 70) can be used to predict your aerobic and anaerobic thresholds, you should cultivate an ability to feel when you are running the right pace in your threshold workouts, since running the right *speed* is only half the intent of these workouts—running the proper *effort* is the other half.

Chapter 3
Physiological Adaptations to Training

Running, or indeed any type of athletic training, induces a range of biological changes in your body that help improve your fitness. Investigating these changes can explain why various types of training have different effects on your performance and, hopefully, can give some insight into how to combine the individual types of training into a complete program.

Elite athletes have been employing high-volume aerobic training for decades. When Arthur Lydiard demonstrated the power of long term aerobic development, little was known about *why* it worked. However, we now know that frequent high-volume and high-quality aerobic running produces specific physiological adaptations in the heart, blood, capillaries, and muscle fibers. Likewise, these same structures respond in different ways to fast anaerobic running. Properly-structured training can target all of these systems to maximize your performance.

Heart Adaptations

Your heart rate remains elevated throughout long bouts of continuous running. In response to this, your heart grows bigger, stronger, and more efficient. During exercise, the heart pumps blood through the lungs and into the muscles, delivering oxygen to the mitochondria. With a stronger heart, you will eventually be able to run at the same pace with a lower heart rate, as your heart will move larger volumes of blood per beat. Correspondingly, your resting heart rate will drop. While a sedentary person's heart might beat at 60 to 80 beats per minute when at rest, some Olympic caliber athletes have resting heart rates as low as 30 beats per minute!

The heart's output during high-intensity exercise can be increased enormously through training. During a maximal effort, like a cross country race, sedentary people have cardiac outputs of less than 20 liters of blood per minute. In contrast, a trained athlete's heart can pump up to 35 liters per minute (imagine filling a two-liter bottle in 3.4 seconds!). A higher maximum cardiac output delivers more oxygen per minute to the muscles, enabling a faster pace in workouts and races.

Lung Adaptations

Surprisingly, there are very few changes in the lungs in response to heavy training. While the strength and endurance of the respiratory muscles increases, there is hardly any change in the structure of the lungs themselves. This indicates that the lungs are not a performance-limiting factor in healthy athletes. The volume and surface area inside the lungs are easily large enough to fully saturate all available red blood cells with oxygen. However, this is not the case at high altitude, where performance drops steadily at elevations above 3200 feet above sea level, and when the airways are obstructed by inflammation, as is the case with exercise-induced asthma—an underdiagnosed problem in runners.

Blood Adaptations

Blood shows one of the most marked reactions to training. In response to aerobic stress on the cardiovascular system, the body releases a hormone called erythropoietin (EPO) from the kidneys into the bloodstream. EPO increases the production of red blood cells, which deliver oxygen to the muscles. More oxygen in the muscles means that more ATP can be produced aerobically, which reduces acid buildup and makes running at a given pace easier.

Oxygen from the lungs binds to iron in a protein called **hemoglobin** which makes up red blood cells. Iron is made available to the body by **ferritin**, an iron-storage protein that circulates freely in the bloodstream. The iron in ferritin ultimately comes from your diet. Without iron, red blood cell production cannot continue. Low iron intake in your diet will cause a decrease in hemoglobin and serum ferritin levels, which will lead to decreased production of red blood cells, and eventually, impaired performance. Even when hemoglobin levels are normal, performance can suffer when your ferritin levels are low, perhaps because iron is also used by other proteins which play a role in the anaerobic energy system. For unknown reasons, ferritin levels below 25 ng/ml have also been reported to be associated with an increase in overuse injuries.

Your blood chemistry also changes in response to fast anaerobic training. In response to the influx of protons, lactate, and the corresponding rise in acidity (see pp. 10-11), the

	Hemoglobin (g/dl)		Serum Ferritin (ng/ml)	
	Sedentary	Athlete	Sedentary	Athlete
Men	14-18	13-18	18-270	25+ (ideally 50+)
Women	12-16	11-16	18-160	25+ (ideally 50+)

Normal hemoglobin and ferritin levels for sedentary males and females compared with normal levels for endurance athletes. Ferritin levels under 25 ng/ml will cause significant drops in performance and possibly increase the risk of injury. You should have your doctor check your iron levels at least once a year.[2, 3]

blood creates enzymes to process byproducts of ATP synthesis and releases buffering agents to guard against a spike in acidity. Interval workouts and races also improve your body's ability to process lactate and shuttle it across cell membranes, which delays acid buildup in the muscles.

Capillary Adaptations

In conjunction with improvements in blood chemistry, the body's vascular system becomes more effective. Blood vessels only a few ten-thousandths of an inch in diameter called **capillaries** grow in size and number, extending deeper into the leg muscles. The growth of the capillaries improves both oxygen delivery and waste removal.

Muscular Adaptations

When exposed to aerobic stress, mitochondria, the "power plants" inside your muscle cells, multiply to process the increased supply of oxygen from the blood. In addition, the muscle fibers themselves strengthen and adapt to training. Though muscle fibers are usually described as being either **fast twitch** or **slow twitch**, there are actually several classes of muscle fibers, ranging from "Type I" to "Type IIX."[4]

Type I muscle fibers are slow twitch, meaning they can efficiently use the aerobic system for very long periods of time, though they cannot contract as fast as the Type II fibers.

Type IIX is a true fast twitch fiber, meaning it can use the anaerobic and phosphocreatine energy systems to create large amounts of power and can fire very rapidly.

Between these two extremes, many muscle fibers are of an intermediate type and can respond to training to become more fast twitch-like or slow twitch-like. As you might guess, exposure to long aerobic training encourages these intermediate fibers to develop slow twitch characteristics, and explosive strength and sprint training causes them to develop fast twitch characteristics.

The Female Athlete Triad

Because of the menstrual cycle, female athletes are much more susceptible to iron deficiency. Iron deficiency in women also contributes to the **Female Athlete Triad**, a condition characterized by insufficient caloric intake, amenorrhea (lack of menstruation), and osteoporosis (low bone density). Disordered eating precipitates all three symptoms. In sedentary or moderately active women, the usual bodily response to insufficient caloric intake is to burn fat, but when body fat reserves are low (as is the case with many female distance runners), the body will go into "survival mode" and conserve energy by weakening the immune system, decreasing available energy, stopping the menstrual cycle, and disrupting the hormones responsible for bone growth and repair. The result is inevitably poor performance, stress fractures and other overuse injuries, anemia, and frequent sickness. Untreated, it can become life-threatening. Persistent underperformance, abnormal fatigue and tiredness, missed periods, injuries, or unexplained bouts of illness may be signs of a serious problem.

In the past, the field of exercise physiology believed that heavy training automatically triggered amenorrhea, but modern research has shown that the true cause is insufficient caloric intake. With a proper diet, women can run over 100 miles per week and still menstruate. Amenorrhea is a red flag that the body is not getting enough fuel and it must be promptly addressed by your coach and doctor.

The adaptability of muscle fibers is part of what allows many runners to be successful at a wide range of events. Although much of muscle fiber composition is genetic, the right training can tailor the intermediate fibers toward your race distances of choice.

Muscle biopsies of elite sprinters show a high proportion of fast twitch fibers, which no doubt enables their explosive speed. Likewise, marathon runners tend to have a much greater percentage of slow twitch muscle fibers. However, because of the versatile intermediate muscle fibers, long-distance prowess does not preclude the ability to close a race with a fast kick, nor does good top speed prevent an athlete from excelling at the longer distances. Elite male 10,000m runners can finish a championship race with a 52 or 53 second last lap, and many 800m and mile specialists also shine brightly in 5, 8, and 10-kilometer cross country races.

Chapter 3 Summary

The most important adaptations to exercise occur in your heart, blood cells, blood vessels, and muscles. Some of these changes, like shifts in muscle fiber composition, can be slow and relatively limited, while others, like improvements in your heart's ability to pump blood, are tremendous. Understanding that these biological structures respond differently to various types of stress (e.g. long aerobic runs vs. fast interval workouts on the track) is important for guiding how you plan out your training.

Chapter 4
Theory into Practice: Targeting Specific Physiological Adaptations

Just like our understanding of the AT and AnT allowed us to specifically target them in training to improve performance, we can also tailor our training to maximize specific physiological adaptations. By ensuring that your training program includes workouts which target all of the biological systems which influence your performance, you can avoid being held back by deficits in your fitness.

However, you must remember that **adequate recovery** is the key to success. Adaptation is the recovery response to a stress; without a recovery period, there is no improvement. Long and fast running causes damage to your body, and the recovery in response to this is the source of improvement.

Target the Oxygen Delivery System

The heart, blood, and capillaries can be collectively referred to as the **oxygen delivery system**, and they all respond similarly to the same types of aerobic stress. They are also the slowest to develop. While maximum cardiac output and blood chemistry can be optimized in 4-8 weeks' time, it takes several months to develop the oxygen delivery system to a high level of fitness. Indeed, it can take *years* of training to reach peak aerobic shape. Further, development of maximum cardiac output, muscle fibers, and blood chemistry is greatly aided by a well-developed oxygen delivery system.

Thankfully, the effects of aerobic training also take a long time to wear off. In contrast, improvements in blood chemistry and maximum cardiac output revert in a matter of weeks. This is why a long period of emphasis on aerobic training is needed before intense anaerobic training and racing are to begin. The frequency, duration, and intensity of aerobic stress on the oxygen delivery system determine the extent of its adaptation.

Frequent exposure to aerobic stress elicits a stronger response. To target this, a young athlete might move from running five or six days a week one season to seven days a week the next. A more experienced runner might double (run twice in one day) four days a week instead of two. Though running twice a day can be an enormous benefit to your fitness, you will have to take care that it does not encroach on your sleep and your recovery. As your running career progresses, you can move towards doubling more often. Top high school runners often double 2-3 times a week during the summer and winter, but cut back as their important races approach. Top college athletes might double 4-5 times a week, continuing to do so even into the racing season. Many elite post-collegiate runners double almost every single day!

Increasing the **duration** of aerobic stress triggers a very strong response from the heart, capillaries, blood, and muscle fibers. Running continuously at easy to moderate paces directly stimulates all of these systems. In addition to your daily training runs, it is beneficial to include a weekly or biweekly **long run** approximately 1½ times further than a "normal" run. Without this, your oxygen delivery system will be underdeveloped. An experienced distance runner training at 80 miles per week might have a long run of about 15-16 miles every Saturday, while a younger runner doing 50 miles per week might run 11-13 miles every other Saturday. Despite the lack of physiological evidence, the pioneering coach Arthur Lydiard of New Zealand recognized the benefits of long runs over fifty years ago and they have been a mainstay of modern training ever since.

The frequency and duration of your runs determine your weekly mileage. While any discussion of mileage is incomplete without talking about intensity, mileage is nevertheless a useful training metric. As you progress in training, your mileage will increase over time. A generally-agreed upon rule is that your peak weekly mileage can increase by around 10-15 miles every year, depending on your experience and your race distances of choice. For example, a high school freshman who ran 30 miles per week over the winter can move to 40 or 45 miles per week as a sophomore. In the short term, it's a good idea to cap any increases in weekly mileage to 10% per week—increasing from 50 miles one week to 55 the next, for example. Hitting new mileage peaks is great, but your ultimate goal should be to maintain *consistent* mileage that is *reasonably* high over many weeks and months.

While your ideal weekly mileage is a highly individual matter, the demands of long-distance races put some basic constraints on how much you need to run. Barring a few outliers with supreme natural talent, it's very hard to succeed in races from 3km on up without a respectable mileage base.

Experience shows that top high school boys tend to run 65-75 miles per week by their senior year, while top high school girls run 45-55 miles per week as seniors. College runners typically run more, both because they are older and more experienced and because their race distances are longer. Top college men usually run from 80 to 100 miles per week as seniors, while top college women tend to run 55-75 miles per week. Successful middle distance runners have a greater range of mileage; some 800m runners do as little as 30 miles per week, while others do 80 or more! Keep these guidelines in mind while also considering your own experiences with differing mileage levels when you plan your long-term training goals.

The **intensity,** or more simply, the speed at which you train, also influences the oxygen delivery system. Workouts at the aerobic or anaerobic threshold are one example of using intensity as a stimulus. However, it is easy to overload on intensity in training. You should aim for an *effort level,* not a specific pace. Runs done at an easy effort should naturally get faster as your fitness improves, but the temptation to *force* the pace is always a threat. It is important to recognize that, as long as you are training at the right effort, you are eliciting the proper training response.

Arthur Lydiard never prescribed paces for training runs, only effort levels. If "1" was an all-out race, most training runs would be at "¼ effort"—an easy, relaxed pace. A few runs would be at "½ effort"—an honest, but still moderate pace. Finally, once a week, he prescribed a run at "¾ effort," a brisk, fast pace which was a bit slower than the aerobic threshold. These were, in effect, an early version of an aerobic threshold run.

A very good rule for applying stress to the oxygen delivery system is ***never* to increase your training volume and training intensity at the same time**. When increasing your weekly mileage, you should keep the effort on all runs very relaxed. After adapting to the increase in volume, you can do some runs at an increased effort, perhaps incorporating progression runs and some aerobic and anaerobic threshold workouts as you grow more comfortable at the new mileage level.

Target Maximum Cardiac Output

Aerobic training, particularly high-end aerobic workouts like AT runs and cruise intervals, strengthens the heart considerably. But to improve your maximum cardiac output, you must spend a significant amount of time at your maximum heart rate. This is best accomplished during the anaero-

Training Your VO$_2$ Max vs. Race-Specific Training

VO$_2$ max workouts are a contentious issue in the coaching world, since the pace does not really correlate to a specific race pace. 3k pace is a tad too fast, while 5k pace is a bit too slow. Many coaches prefer to prescribe race-specific workouts, not worrying whether the pace is exactly at the VO$_2$ max or not. Indeed, your VO$_2$ max seems to plateau after a few years of training—after that, most improvement comes from gains in efficiency. But even if you don't believe in running VO$_2$ max pace for its own sake, every runner should do *some* work at 3k or 5k pace. Pure middle-distance runners require endurance work in that pace range, and long-distance specialists ought not to forget how to move fast. For 3k and 5k runners, of course, most race-pace training is right around VO$_2$ max pace anyway. Experienced runners may opt for shorter repeats of 300-600m in the 3k-5k pace range with short to moderate recovery periods to improve efficiency while avoiding the taxing acidosis that comes along with traditional VO$_2$ max work.

bic development phase of your training cycle. When your heart is beating at its maximum rate, your oxygen delivery system is operating at its absolute limit. This is called your **VO$_2$ max**—you are consuming the maximum volume (V) of oxygen (O$_2$) that you can. The slowest pace which elicits your VO$_2$ max falls somewhere in between 5000m and 3000m race pace. Any increase in pace beyond this level simply relies on the anaerobic system to provide the additional energy. So, to spend the most amount of time running at your maximum heart rate, you want to run as slow as possible while still at your VO$_2$ max. Any faster, and you will simply get more fatigued without getting a better cardiac training response.

The best type of training for improving your maximum cardiac output (and therefore VO$_2$ max) is an interval workout with several repeats lasting 2-5 minutes at around 3000m to 5000m race pace with roughly equal recovery. The total time spent running at VO$_2$ max pace should be between 15 and 20 minutes. These workouts tend to be quite strenuous, so it is important to be cautious. It's far better to run within your means, not doing so many repeats that you end the workout doubled over and gasping for air. Such workouts tend to require more than the usual day of easy running to recover from and are not conducive to learning to run efficiently.

Target Blood Chemistry

The release of EPO into the bloodstream (and the corresponding increase in red blood cells) responds proportionally to the frequency, duration, and intensity of aerobic running, so it can be thought of as part of the oxygen delivery system. However, training the bloodstream to handle the heavy influx of protons and lactate which occurs during middle and long-distance races requires a specialized and more conservative stress and recovery strategy.

As mentioned in the description of the anaerobic energy system, a hard interval workout or race will release a large amount of acid into the blood, overwhelming the body's buffering system and causing acidosis. The body usually needs at least a 48 hour recovery period to restore internal balance, release more enzymes to aid anaerobic performance, and be prepared for another hard effort.

While from a blood chemistry standpoint, the pace and structure of your workouts are not overly important, these factors strongly influence muscle and nerve development, so in general it is best to target paces at, above, and below your goal race pace. So, during the anaerobic development or "pace" phase of training, after building up a base of aerobic fitness but before the most important competitions, a miler's race-specific interval training would be composed of three types of workouts: short repeats at faster than race pace (perhaps 800m race pace) with long recovery for speed, medium-length repeats at mile pace with moderate recovery for stamina, and longer repeats at slower paces (3k, 5k, and possibly 10k pace) with short recovery for endurance. While long-distance runners can do more absolute workout volume, middle-distance runners can run larger volumes relative to their race distance: a 10k runner might do 8 or 10km of race-specific work (10x1km, for example), while a miler could do 6x500m, which totals almost twice his or her race distance. Most of the time, faster and more difficult repeats should be accompanied by longer recovery periods because they generate exponentially more metabolic waste, which requires extra time to remove from the blood and muscles.

Many runners glorify ultra-difficult, gut-churning interval workouts as the secret to big improvements. But in reality, otherworldly interval sessions do little to improve your fitness. Your body has a limited capability to recovery, and when a workout exceeds this, you will struggle just to maintain your initial fitness after such a strenuous workload.

When you read about top runners cranking out unreal training sessions, it is more often a reflection of the fitness they *already have*—fitness garnered through aerobic development and more moderate workouts. For this reason, "classic" workouts like 10x400m at mile pace or 5xmile at 5k pace can be counterproductive simply because the *workout* becomes

Speed	12x200m at 800m pace, 60-90sec recovery 4x400m at 800m pace, 5-6min recovery
Stamina	2*7x300m at mile pace, 60sec b/t reps, 4min b/t sets 6x500m at mile pace, 3-4min recovery 3x800m at mile pace, 8-10min recovery
Endurance	5x800m at 3k pace, 3min recovery 6x1000m at 5k pace, 3min recovery 3-4x2000m at 10k pace, 3min recovery

Possible interval workouts for a miler. The range of paces improves **speed** at faster than race pace, **stamina** at race pace, and **endurance** at slower than race pace. For more sample workouts, see Appendix C (p. 74).

more important than the *race*. It takes a truly disciplined runner to ignore split times over such familiar distances. Far more runners can do ten 64-second 400s with a minute of recovery than can run a 4:16 mile—more abstract distances like 300m or 500m can help reconnect the workout with its intended purpose. Genuinely helpful interval sessions are the ones that teach you to run your race pace more **relaxed**, not more **aggressively**.

Training anaerobically more than two or three times a week, whether to target blood chemistry, VO_2 max, or race-specific fitness, will not allow your body to return to normal and will sap energy from the neuromuscular system, altering hormone levels, and leading to chronic acidity in the blood. This condition is known as **overtraining** or **burnout**. Workouts will be sluggish and races will be lackluster; you will feel constantly tired and you will be more susceptible to illness and injury. The physical and mental effects of burnout can ruin a season. To combat this, all modern training programs worth their salt will separate hard workouts with at least one day of easy aerobic running. The benefits of this are twofold: it helps flush out any toxic remnants of the previous day's hard effort, and it also keeps the oxygen delivery system in good shape.

Legendary University of Oregon coach Bill Bowerman was a strong proponent of the **hard-easy philosophy**—separating hard efforts with days of easy aerobic running to allow the body to recover and improve. Though there's nothing wrong with occasionally turning an "easy" run into a spontaneous faster run during base training when you're feeling good, it's better to keep the effort easy on *all* of your runs once you have begun to do difficult workouts.

Overtraining is not only a risk during anaerobic development. A surprising number of runners overtrain by forcing a hard pace when they are targeting the oxygen delivery system in the base phase of training. While occasional and targeted intensity is a great thing for your aerobic fitness, you

The Importance of Recovery

Kenny Moore, one of Bill Bowerman's athletes in the 1960s, was constantly getting sick or injured even on Bowerman's hard-easy program. Bowerman, seeing this, convinced Moore to take *two* easy days between hard efforts. He adopted a nine-day training schedule, which included long intervals, short intervals, and a long run, each separated by two easy days. An easy day consisted of a 3 to 5 mile jog in the morning and another easy 3 to 5 miles in the evening. With very few modifications, this training program would eventually take him all the way to a 4th-place finish in the 1972 Olympic marathon, with fellow American Frank Shorter taking first.

Photo courtesy Bruce Mortenson and Kenny Moore

need adequate recovery during base training too—a good number of your runs should be at an easy pace. This same aggressive attitude can cause runners to take on too hefty of a training regimen, piling strength, strides, and mileage onto an already-full work or school schedule, inevitably sacrificing sleep, recovery, and nutrition. If you start to feel the effects of overtraining, stop any longer or faster running and do short, easy jogging for several days until you feel recovered. Cut back on ancillary training like weight lifting and plyometrics, and ensure that you are getting enough sleep, fluids, and calories in your diet.

Target Muscle Fibers

The same high-volume aerobic training that stimulates the oxygen delivery system is also well-suited for developing slow twitch muscle fibers and encouraging the growth of mitochondria. But targeting fast twitch muscle fibers is best accomplished by long runs, hills, and a routine of plyometric strength exercises.

During normal aerobic running, only slow twitch muscle fibers are activated. The fast twitch muscle fibers are typically reserved for fast anaerobic running. However, the fast twitch fibers are recruited during aerobic runs when the incline or duration exceeds the power limit of the slow twitch fibers. A steep hill demands more power than slow twitch fibers alone can deliver, so the fast twitch fibers kick in to help. Likewise, a long run of 90-120 minutes depletes the glucose stored in the slow twitch muscle fibers, forcing the fast twitch fibers to donate their stored energy. It would follow, then, that the best way to strengthen and train *all* muscle fibers would be a long run of 1½-2 hours through hilly terrain. Given this, it is no surprise why Arthur Lydiard's athletes, who would run for two hours every Sunday through the rugged New Zealand hills, were so well-conditioned.

Lydiard also recommended a specific "hill phase" to follow the "marathon conditioning" base phase, which involved workouts of running, skipping, and bounding up steep inclines to strengthen the legs. He did not know this at the time, but these explosive, dynamic hill bounding exercises are examples of what we now call **plyometrics**. Instead of the slow movement or static resistance provided by weight machines, the explosive nature of plyometrics mimics muscle motion while running and increases efficiency and top speed. Power-skipping, bounding, scissor kicks, and single-leg hops are examples of explosive plyometric exercises that can strengthen your legs and lead to a more powerful, efficient stride.

The specifics of designing a plyometric strengthening program are beyond the scope of this book (see p. 68 for some resources on plyometrics), but when choosing strength exercises, keep in mind the **principle of specificity**: "The body becomes good at what it practices." Remember, training is *means to an end*, and that end is running fast. Your strength-

Barefoot Running and Racing Flats

In an ideal world, we would have been born and raised on miles of warm, grassy, well-maintained trails and would never have needed shoes to run. However, because of the abundance of pavement and broken glass in modern society (not to mention winter weather), plus the fact that we have become accustomed to wearing shoes all day, we train in running shoes on asphalt and concrete—or dirt and gravel if we're lucky. Modern shoe technology has allowed many people to overcome injuries and biomechanical defects that would otherwise prevent them from training at a high level.

However, the trade-off for stability and cushioning in our shoes is strength and range of motion in our feet and ankles, as well as sloppier running form and lower stride frequencies. Recently, doing a few miles of barefoot running on grass every week has become a popular way to strengthen muscles and tendons in the foot and ankle, and it may help prevent injury too, though this has yet to be proven scientifically.

In addition, many athletes and coaches, especially at the highest levels of competition, feel that it is necessary to run fast workouts in lightweight, less-structured shoes called racing flats to get a full range of motion in the lower legs and ankles. However, the calf muscles and Achilles tendon will not be accustomed to working through their full range of motion, so any barefoot running or workouts in flats should be introduced gradually.

ening exercises should be as similar to actual running as possible. Skipping forward is better than skipping in place. Forward bounding is better than side-to-side bounding. Explosive leg strength is far more valuable than explosive arm strength, and plyometric strengthening is generally superior to slow movements with weights, though a base of general strength is necessary before beginning plyometrics—jumping right in to high-impact exercises can cause injury. Ultimately, the most "specific" plyometric exercise is fast or uphill running! A final caveat: focus on running first; plyometric strength is extra. An hour of running is much better for improving your fitness than half an hour of running plus half an hour of plyometrics.

Staying Strong

Though Arthur Lydiard abhorred the idea of distance runners lifting weights, his colleague and friend Bill Bowerman noted that Lydiard's runners kept themselves strong by doing chores in the countryside like repairing fences, chopping wood, and mixing concrete. With the conveniences of modern life, it is unlikely that your daily activities will keep you strong enough to endure the rigors of training. Today, all elite runners do some type of strength work as a part of their training regimen.

Perhaps because many high schoolers become distance runners after realizing that they aren't particularly athletic in more popular sports, track and cross country runners have a tendency to be weak and uncoordinated. This can leave them vulnerable to overuse injuries and hampers the development of good running form too. You should think of yourself as an athlete, not just a runner! For both performance and injury prevention, it is *extremely* important to build overall muscular strength and endurance, especially in the smaller muscles of the hip, buttocks, and abdomen, by doing targeted exercises like crunches, planks, push-ups, and leg-lifts. Again, a full general strength program won't be covered here, but a good place to start is Jay Johnson's eight-week general strength progression (see p. 68).

Chapter 4 Summary

Through targeted training, the body's range of physiological systems can be tuned for optimal performance. The heart, blood cells, and blood vessels—collectively referred to as the oxygen delivery system—respond strongly to aerobic training. This can be modulated by adjusting the frequency, duration, and intensity of your running. Blood chemistry and maximum cardiac output, two factors that heavily influence your race times, are best targeted through interval workouts at, above, and below the pace of your primary race distance. While long, hilly runs can bolster the endurance of your muscle fibers, general strength and plyometric exercises are useful ancillary training tools to improve your muscular power, speed, and efficiency. Finally, the element that underpins improvements in all of these systems is adequate recovery between training sessions.

Chapter 5
Your Mental Approach

Up until this point, we have focused almost exclusively on the physiological aspects of training. However, as you well know, the body is not a simple running machine. The brain and body interact during exercise in complicated ways. Despite all the physiology we have learned, a biologically less fit runner can still prevail on race day. All the numbers—VO_2 max, cardiac output, muscular composition—can be stacked against you and yet you can still win. In addition, you may struggle to maintain 7:30 miles on a training run one day, but cruise along at under six-minute pace the next. Again, we have no good explanation for this. However, as Lydiard's athletes illustrated in the '60s, we do not need to wait for science to explain everything we do in training.

For example, consider training at the aerobic threshold. A higher AT allows an athlete to feel better running at a given pace. But if he or she is still running with an aggressive mindset, that given pace will still feel too difficult to maintain, *even at a higher fitness level*. **Relaxation** during difficult workouts and races may seem counterintuitive, but it is a strategy employed by the best athletes in the world.

The faces of elite runners do not show strain in a race until the final drive for the finish (and sometimes not even then—observe the calm, serene expression of 1:44 800m runner Tyler Mulder on the far left of this book's cover). This is not only a testament to their fitness, but to their ability to eliminate all unnecessary stress on their body—both physical and mental. Athletes who start out from the gun with thoughts of pain and toughness inevitably expend too much energy in the first half of a race, struggling home out of contention. An aggressive mindset is not only mentally draining, but contributes to a tense and inefficient stride, robbing you of real, physical energy. Save "guts" for when you need it: the *last* part of a distance race.

For the same reasons, you should run most of your workouts with the intention of practicing smooth, efficient, and relaxed running. This should be reflected both in your mindset and in your times. Putting an overly aggressive effort into your workouts or running them too fast only trains your body to get tired. If anything, your split times should get gradually faster throughout the course of a workout. Remember, the whole goal of training is to be able to run fast *without*

Viola Kibiwot, Meseret Defar, and Tirunesh Dibaba running relaxed and focused at the 2012 Olympic 5000m. These women would go on to win the bronze, silver, and gold medals, respectively. *Photo: Nick J Webb*

The 800m: A pacing peculiarity

For every race from 1500m up to the marathon, even or slightly negative splits are the best way to run a PR. Lap times from national and world records reflect this—the most economical way to run is with each lap being the same speed as the last, or perhaps slightly faster near the end of the race. But in the 800m, most records are set with the second lap being around two seconds slower than the first. One reason for this may be that the phosphocreatine system, which provides a significant portion of the first lap's effort, helps reduce acidity in the muscle cells, buying time before fatigue sets in. Coaching experience shows that, from the high school junior varsity level all the way up to the Olympics, half-milers should expect their first lap to be two or *maybe* three seconds faster than their second. Of course, the brevity of the 800m is extremely unforgiving. A slight miscalculation in pace can lead to the second lap being *several* seconds slower than the first, which is both frustrating and painful!

getting fatigued! Now, you'll obviously have some difficult workouts, and mental tricks won't make them effortless. But approaching these with a relaxed and focused mindset makes getting through the workout a simple matter of completing the task at hand, allowing you to dodge the discouraging effects of a bad workout caused by running too fast or too aggressively.

In the same vein, building speed is not about running *hard*. Short, relaxed, fast repetitions, often called "**strides**," should be employed at least twice a week during all phases of training to learn to run quickly, efficiently, and smoothly. You can even run these on a gradual downhill occasionally in a further effort to teach your body to run quickly with little effort. Again, just like training the AT and AnT, *forcing* the pace or trying to sprint *aggressively* while doing strides is counterproductive. To keep strides light and efficient, they should not result in acidosis. Correspondingly, they should not last longer than about 35 seconds and should have plenty of recovery.

Doing 6x100m starting at 5000m race pace and descending to one mile or 800m race pace by the final repeat with an easy jog back to the start after each is an excellent way to improve speed and can be done after a normal training run or before a workout several times a week, even during base training. The principle of specificity applies again here: train as close to racing conditions as you can. So, if you are preparing for cross country, do your strides on grass in cross country spikes. Using your racing shoes also encourages a full range of motion through the ankle and foot.

Many runners and coaches will blame a poor race performance on "not being tough enough," but often, the athlete's lap splits tell a different story. Starting out a race too fast, taking the lead too early, or putting erratic pace surges into the middle of a race are three surefire ways to drain the mental and physical energy that you'll need to finish strong. Almost every distance world record has been set with even or slightly negative splits, and top runners know to bide their time waiting behind another runner before taking the lead. Of course, *somebody* has to lead the race, but when considering whether or not you should move to the front of the pack, be aware of the costs associated with it: not only is following another runner mentally easier, but the lessened air resistance will make your pace about one second per 400m easier—even on a perfectly calm day!

When preparing for a big race, it's easy to forget everything you've learned and make some novice mistakes, or psych yourself out and spend all of your energy *worrying* about the race instead of actually running it. Training yourself to keep calm, relax, and carry out your race plan in an important competition is a skill that can take many years to cultivate, and you shouldn't be surprised if you have some setbacks along the way.

Chapter 5 Summary

Just like real physical training, there are no quick mental tricks for success. Fortunately, the same type of workouts that teach your body to efficiently run fast—high volume, high-end aerobic work, complimented by strides and somewhat challenging (but not overly taxing) race-specific workouts—also teach your mind to stay relaxed while running fast, but *only* when you approach your training with the right mindset. In workouts and races, focus on being <u>relaxed</u> and running *efficiently*, not being <u>aggressive</u> and running *hard*. Finally, efficient running is only possible if you practice efficient pacing, both in workouts and in races.

Chapter 6
Improving Running Economy

What makes the East Africans so fast? That is a question with no clear answer and a storm of controversy surrounding it, but **running economy** plays a significant role. Not all athletes have "perfect" form, but the very best rarely have any wasted movement. Every ounce of exertion is going towards moving their bodies forward. A study of elite Kenyan and Scandinavian athletes found no difference in their VO_2 max, though the Kenyans used much less oxygen at a given pace than the Scandinavians (incidentally, the Kenyans also had faster PRs).[5] This means, though both groups had equal oxygen delivery systems, the Kenyan runners had better running economy. Because their stride was more efficient, they could move faster using the same amount of oxygen.

Many visitors to Kenyan training camps are surprised by the amount of time spent on **form drills**. Also known as **sprint drills** or **dynamics**, these exercises include fast skipping, high knees, and backwards running. Some sprint drills exaggerate a specific aspect of the gait cycle and train the body to do it correctly—that is, waste less energy—while others, like backwards running, enhance joint range of motion and improve coordination. Sprint drills are best learned in person from a good instructor. Sprint athletes and coaches are well-versed in form drills and are an invaluable resource for the budding distance runner.

A sprinter in the 100m dash focuses on making every stride perfect. In that sense, distance runners should aspire to be "slow sprinters": in the 5000m, an athlete will take over 2,500

Sample Sprint Drill Routine
The following sprint drills are a good place to start if you have not developed your own drill routine. Each drill can be done once or twice for 10-25m with a few seconds' rest before beginning the next one. This routine can be done before strides, workouts, and races.

–High-knees
–"As" (down-skipping)
–"Bs" (walking leg kick-outs)
–Skipping "Bs"
–Backwards running
–High skipping
–Carioca (leg crossover)

strides. If every one of these takes five thousandths of a second (0.005 sec) less to execute, a runner will shave 12.5 seconds off of his or her time—a commanding victory in championship races decided by a photo-finish. Plyometrics, uphill running, strength exercises, and strides, detailed in chapters four and five, also help improve running economy by fostering development of a quick, explosive footstrike.

In contrast, if your stride length is too long for a given pace, your foot lands too far in front of your body, which transmits shock up your leg and causes braking forces that slow you down. This is called **overstriding**. The ideal stride is light, quick, and effortless—you should avoid "reaching" forward with your lower leg to increase your stride length. Instead, most of your power should come from driving off the ground with your hips. Your foot will land closer to your body and you will waste less energy overcoming the braking force generated when you overstride.

Steve Magness, former scientific advisor and coach at the Nike Oregon Project, advocates imagining the lower leg being completely relaxed while swinging through the air and simply "unfolding" underneath the body like a pendulum.

Your shin should not be extended out in front of your body with a straight knee at footstrike, as is common with many hobby joggers, but should be just past perpendicular to the ground, with your knee slightly bent to facilitate a quick footstrike.

An easy way to ensure you are not overstriding is to check your stride frequency. Jack Daniels, one of the main proponents of AnT training, has also investigated the stride frequency of elite distance runners. They tend to take 180 strides per minute or more, even at slow paces. In contrast, slower, more injury-prone runners tend to have a bouncy, slow stride instead of a light and efficient one. Sprint drills, strides, and simply trying to match the stride rate of an efficient runner for a while can gradually increase your stride frequency and improve your running economy. A faster stride frequency means that you are spending less time on the ground; furthermore, your body has to absorb less shock per footstrike. An easy way to check your stride frequency is to count how many times your right leg hits the ground in 30 seconds and multiply by four.

Recently, much attention has been paid to your **footstrike**, or where your foot actually hits the ground when you run, but there is no good evidence that any type of footstrike results in superior performance or fewer injuries. If anything, footstrike styles appear to merely influence where forces are directed in the body, with forefoot striking increasing forces through the foot, ankle, calf, and Achilles, and heel striking increasing forces through the heel, shin, and knee. Altering footstrike is rather drastic, so most runners should avoid it.

Like with sprint drills, a distance runner can gain a lot by learning from sprinters when it comes to running form. Powerful hips, minimizing wasted energy, and avoiding overstriding have been fundamental pieces of sprint coaching for decades, but it is only recently that distance runners have taken note. Like all new things in training, any change in running form should be small and gradual.

Chapter 6 Summary

Running economy is a measurement of how efficiently your body converts the oxygen it consumes into forward motion. Athletes with good running economy can run at faster speeds while requiring less energy (and hence incurring less acid buildup) than runners with an inefficient stride. Incorporating sprint drills and checking your stride frequency are two very good ways to improve your form. Building a light, quick, and efficient stride is a gradual process, but the payoffs extend to all areas of your training.

Chapter 7
Planning a Season

While a lot has changed since the 1960s, Arthur Lydiard's basic approach, consisting of a 10-12 week "base building" or "marathon conditioning" phase, followed by 4-8 weeks of anaerobic, race-specific training prior to your most important competitions, still reigns supreme. The human body seems to operate best on a **training cycle** lasting about six months: a **base phase** of 10-12 weeks (or more) of relaxed, high-volume aerobic training, followed by a 4-8 week **anaerobic development phase** which emphasizes race-specific workouts and low-key racing, and finally, a **racing phase** of several weeks with important races.

Too many high school and college programs are eager to neglect the base phase in favor of doing hard workouts and races all year, limiting their athletes' long-term aerobic development. Racing year-round is counterproductive not only because it is mentally and physically draining, but because it prevents you from establishing solid aerobic conditioning, the cornerstone of your fitness.

In each six-month training cycle (for most high school and college runners, June-November and December-May), you should dedicate two to three months to improving your oxygen delivery system through higher mileage and high-end aerobic workouts like AT runs, cruise intervals, AnT runs, and progression runs. While you could do a road race or two for fun during the base phase, frequent racing will inhibit good training. If you are a coach, keep this in mind when considering your team's racing schedule—it's no accident that many of the top high school programs around the country come from states without lengthy indoor track seasons or summer racing circuits!

As the racing season approaches, your training should transition from the base phase to the anaerobic development phase. During this period, you will begin to incorporate race-specific interval workouts into your weekly schedule to hone your fitness. Athletes need differing amounts of anaerobic work before they are ready to race their best; runners who take well to aerobic training might only need 3-4 race-specific workouts before they are ready to compete well, while others (especially middle distance runners) might need several weeks' worth of race-specific work. To keep different runners on a similar racing schedule, you can swap out race-specific workouts with high-end aerobic workouts and easy runs or vice versa to modulate the balance of aerobic and anaerobic training in your schedule.

Renato Canova, a world-renowned Italian coach who works with many of the elite Kenyan and Ethiopian runners, says that "training is not to replace, but to ADD"—that is, as you transition from one phase of training to the next, you do not *replace* old workouts with new ones, but instead *add* to your pool of available workouts to choose from. Much in the same way, individual workouts can be modified or added to as you progress in training: a 5mi moderate run can become a 5mi AT run, or a 6x1000m workout can become 7x1000m or 4x1500m.

Workouts during the various phases do not have to be *exclusively* of one type. During all phases of training, you should always touch on your strengths. For a long-distance specialist, this is aerobic endurance—long, continuous running at high-end aerobic speeds. For a middle-distance runner, this is speed endurance—short to moderate repeats at fairly fast speeds with good efficiency and relaxation. So, a middle distance runner might occasionally do some relaxed speed-work like a dozen or so 200s at 3k to mile pace even during the base phase, and a long-distance runner shouldn't neglect periodic high-end aerobic work, even during the anaerobic development and racing phases. Rather, you should *emphasize* base for two or three months, then *emphasize* race-pace workouts for a month or two, and finally put your hard work to use during the racing phase.

During the anaerobic development phase, a long-distance specialist would continue high-end aerobic work begun during the base phase, supplementing it with some race-specific interval workouts at 3k, 5k, or 10k pace, while a middle-distance specialist would gravitate towards higher speeds and intensity, returning only once every week or two to the high-end aerobic workouts that are the bread and butter of the base phase. Doing some low-key races is also desirable (and often necessary) during the anaerobic development phase, but be careful not to overdo it; recognize that racing can be thought of as a highly taxing race-specific workout, so if you race *and* do race-specific workouts too frequently, you'll be overworking yourself.

When it comes to **peaking**, or how and when to reduce volume and increase intensity near the end of the season as the most important races approach, there is vigorous disagreement in the coaching world. Some coaches, like Joe Vigil of Adams State fame, advocate a very aggressive decrease in volume (dropping to as much as half or a third of your training cycle's maximum volume) and doing interval workouts that are much shorter and faster. Others, like acclaimed coaches Scott Simmons and Will Freeman, believe that hardly any change in normal training is necessary. Their athletes run nearly their peak mileage the week of their regional and national meets, with only a small change in workout volume and no change in workout speeds. The majority of coaches and runners fall somewhere between these two extremes, but you will have to find out for yourself what works best for you and your team.

Through my own running experience, I've tended to lean towards the Simmons/Freeman philosophy. If your training has been working well for most of the season, why take a gamble by drastically changing it at the end? Regardless, it's hard to argue with the success of the many coaches who use very drastic or aggressive "tapers" for their athletes. Peaking is an individual aspect of training that you'll have to experiment with. Whatever your approach, you will likely have a 4-6 week period where you are in prime racing shape, so you should fit this window around your most important competitions. If you continue to race frequently, your aerobic conditioning will start to deteriorate and affect your performance, necessitating another base phase to being the training cycle for the next season's races.

Depending on your own personal training philosophy, you may want to include transitional periods at the junction of the different phases in training. Lydiard, for example, liked to include a 4-week "coordination phase" between the anaerobic development phase and the racing phase so athletes could transition from more general anaerobic work to race-specific speeds and distances. Many modern coaches like to have transitional periods between the base phase and anaerobic development phase where runners gradually incorporate more race-specific interval training. A week or two of rest at the end of a training cycle before the next one begins is also popular.

Chapter 7 Summary

Training is best designed in six-month cycles, consisting of a base phase lasting 10-12 weeks to develop aerobic fitness, followed by an anaerobic development phase of 4-8 weeks which focuses on developing race-specific fitness with interval workouts and low-key races, and finally a racing phase of 4-6 weeks where the main focus is being well-prepared for the most important competitions of the season. Each training phase does not need to focus *exclusively* on one aspect of fitness; rather, they should be thought of as periods of *emphasis*. During all phases of training, you'll want to at least touch on your strengths and weaknesses. For some examples on how to plan workouts for a training cycle, see Appendix C (p. 74).

Chapter 8
Nutrition and Body Size

A balanced diet is important for success in all sports, and the basics are well-known—whole grains, lean protein, healthy fats, and plenty of fruits and vegetables. But distance runners need to pay particular attention to their carbohydrate, protein, calcium, and iron intake. What follows is some basic information on a few of the most overlooked aspects of the diet of a distance runner.

Carbohydrates provide the raw fuel for athletes in training. Many runners do not consume enough carbohydrates to fully replenish their muscular energy stores between workouts. A study of elite Kenyan athletes found that a stunning 71% of their daily calories were from carbohydrates.[6] As we discussed in chapter one, a large amount of the energy used while running comes directly from glucose. Glucose is nothing more than a simple form of sugar, which comes straight from your dietary carbohydrate intake.

Protein is essential for repairing the damage done to muscles in a workout or training run. Insufficient protein intake is often a concern in women, where it can contribute to overtraining and the female athlete triad (see sidebar, p. 29). Eating a snack with protein and carbohydrates within 15 minutes following a workout and before going to bed will go a long ways towards boosting recovery.

Calcium protects and strengthens the bones. After a workout, there are spots of microscopic damage on the surface of your bones. During a recovery period, your body repairs and strengthens these areas using calcium from your diet. Vitamin D, either from food or from exposure to sunlight, is also needed because it boosts calcium absorption and contributes to bone growth. A 2007 study found that supplementing the diet of female US Navy recruits with 200% of their recommended daily intake for calcium and 150% for vitamin D decreased the risk of a stress fracture by 25%, and other research has found that females runners who get stress fractures have low dietary calcium intake.[7, 8] While supplementation is not necessary for most runners, it is a good idea to ensure you are getting enough calcium and vitamin D in your diet from dairy, green leafy vegetables, fish, and exposure to sunlight.

Finally, **iron** intake from red meat and other sources enables your body to produce red blood cells. All distance athletes should have their serum ferritin and hemoglobin levels checked yearly and should take an iron supplement if recommended by their physician (see pp. 27-28 for more on iron levels). Like vitamin D and calcium, **vitamin C** boosts iron absorption. One important note: calcium competes with iron for absorption, so consuming both at the same time will hamper your body's ability to absorb the iron.

Racing Weight and Body Size

A recent trend in the running world has been a fixation with body size and "racing weight"— the belief that runners should slim down as much as possible to fit a big "engine" (heart, lungs, and blood vessels) in a smaller body, hopefully improving performance on race day. But the problem with this idea is that weight loss often goes hand-in-hand with muscle loss, especially when it's done in a forced manner. By sharply restricting your caloric intake and maintaining your training workload, you may drop a few pounds, but you will be losing strength as well, not to mention interfering with your body's ability to repair itself.

Alarmingly, this trend also pushes many runners—especially women—towards disordered eating, which can have a huge impact on both your training and your overall health. The very idea that smaller is always better is quite suspect. There are several world-class athletes who never got the memo that they weren't supposed to run fast. Erin Donohue, at 5'7 and 143 pounds, powered her way to a spot on the 2008 Olympic team at 1500m and has run a 4:28 mile. And apparently nobody told Chris Solinsky, who stands 6'1 and weighs 165 pounds, that he was too heavy to become the first American to break 27 minutes in the 10,000m.

4:28 miler and 2008 Olympian Erin Donohue isn't your stereotypical rail-thin runner. *Photo: Victor Sailer, PhotoRun.net*

Instead of focusing on weight, it's best to focus on training well and eating well. With a good training program and healthy meals, your body will gradually adapt to its ideal size and composition (which may differ from that of other runners!). Worries of bulking up with strength work are unfounded, as distance training inhibits large gains in muscle mass. Bodybuilders and weight lifters actually *avoid* aerobic training for this reason. In the end, only two numbers matter: your time and your place!

Chapter 8 Summary

What you eat provides the fuel you need to train and recover well. There's no food, diet, or supplement that will transform your running, but by eating healthy foods and taking care that you get enough nutrients—particularly carbohydrates, protein, calcium, and iron—you'll ensure that your body isn't being held back by inadequate nutrition. And though you might hear a lot about "racing weight," the best approach both for health and for running fitness is eating healthy and training well, *not* stressing your body with rapid, forced weight loss.

Chapter 9
Closing Remarks

This book is the result of being a "student of the sport" myself for many years. I have tried to distill the knowledge I have gained and make it understandable to coaches and young, up-and-coming runners. However, there is very little information in the previous pages that is *essential* to success. This is, after all, only "modern training." Ron Clarke became the first man to run 10,000m in under 28 minutes in 1965 neither knowing nor caring about mitochondrial density or his VO_2 max. I can summarize the essence of training for distance runners in three simple points:

1. Listen to your Body

Listening to your body means recovering properly from workouts. It means backing off the pace when your legs are feeling beat up. It means taking care of any injures as soon as they come up—if it hurts to run, *stop running*. It means eating right, getting eight hours of sleep or more every night, and avoiding anything that will significantly impair your performance. It also means running strong when you feel good! And breaking a few of the "rules" about training every once in a while. There are no *real* absolutes in this sport.

2. Train Smart

Notice that this doesn't say "train hard." You could run 400m repeats at mile pace every day, and you'd be training pretty hard. But you wouldn't improve, and it wouldn't be *smart*. Training smart means doing what you need for long-term improvement. It means focusing on aerobic development by intelligently and gradually increasing your weekly mileage, perhaps introducing doubles a few times a week, and going a bit further on your long runs. It means running at a strong aerobic effort a few times every week, as well as working to build a light, quick, and efficient stride. It also means keeping your body strong through a comprehensive strength program so you can stay healthy.

Finally, it involves figuring out what works best for you. While the general principles of training apply to most everyone, your own specific training needs are unique and different from everyone else's, and you can only uncover the "perfect formula" by trial and error.

How many miles should you run per week, and at what pace? What precipitates your injuries? What kind of workouts suit you best? I can't answer any of these questions definitively, and neither can anyone else. You must figure it out yourself. Keeping a good running log will be a great aid, as it allows you to review your training and racing over the years.

3. Love Running

Running should be primarily an enjoyable experience. A quick ten miler in the morning followed by five easy miles in the evening may not sound enjoyable right now, but like many things in training, it will grow on you. If there is any "secret" to running, it is that big improvements come from learning to run *fast* **without** running *hard*, and the high-end aerobic work that teaches you to do this is thoroughly enjoyable. Ultimately, your goal should be good, consistent training over many weeks, months, and years. Learn to love all aspects of your training and *especially* learn to love racing. After a race, either a good one or a bad one, congratulate your competitors and thank the officials. Covering long distances at great speeds is a rare and fleeting joy. Be thankful for it.

Recommended Reading

The aerobic and anaerobic thresholds
- <u>Daniels' Running Formula, Second Edition</u> by Jack Daniels, Ph.D.
  Human Kinetics, 2005

Aerobic training
- Arthur Lydiard, "Athletic Training," edited by Nobby Hashizume.
  http://lydiardfoundation.org/pdfs/al_training.pdf

High-end aerobic running and the mind-body connection

- John Kellogg, "JK Speaks: Progressing to Peak Fitness."
  http://www.letsrun.com/2005/jkfitness.php

Running economy, plyometrics, and general strength
- <u>High-Powered Plyometrics</u> by James Radcliffe and Robert Farentinos.
  Human Kinetics, 1999

- <u>Road to the Top</u> by Joe Vigil.
  Creative Designs, 1995

- Jay Johnson, "Eight Week General Strength Progression."
  http://www.coachjayjohnson.com/2011/11/eight-week-general-strength-progression/

- <u>Run Strong</u> by Kevin Beck.
  Human Kinetics, 2005

References

1. Robergs, R. A., Biochemistry of exercise-induced metabolic acidosis. *AJP: Regulatory, Integrative and Comparative Physiology* **2004,** 287 (3), R502-R516.

2. Hess, J. Iron depletion. http://www.trackandfieldnews.com/hs/coachscorner/20051215.html

3. Pfitzinger, P. Iron for Runners. http://www.pfitzinger.com/labreports/iron.shtml

4. Andersen, J. L.; Aagaard, P., Effects of strength training on muscle fiber types and size; consequences for athletes training for high-intensity sport. *Scandinavian Journal of Medicine & Science in Sports* **2010,** 20, 32-38.

5. Saltin, B.; Larsen, H.; Terrados, N.; Bangsbo, J.; Bak, T.; Kim, C.; Svedenhag, J.; Rolf, C., Aerobic exercise capacity at sea level and at altitude in Kenyan boys, junior and senior runners compared with Scandinavian runners. *Medicine & Science in Sports & Exercise* **2007,** 5 (4), 209-221.

6. Christensen, D. L.; van Hall, G.; Hambraeus, L., Food and macronutrient intake of male adolescent Kalenjin runners in Kenya. *British Journal of Nutrition* **2007,** 88 (06), 711.

7. Lappe, J.; Cullen, D.; Haynatzki, G.; Recker, R.; Ahlf, R.; Thompson, K., Calcium and vitamin D supplementation decreases incidence of stress fractures in female navy recruits. *Journal of Bone and Mineral Research* **2008,** 23 (5), 741-749.

8. Kelsey, J. L.; Bachrach, L. K.; Procter-Gray, E.; Nieves, J.; Greendale, G. A.; Sowers, M.; Brown, B. W.; Matheson, K. A.; Crawford, S. L.; Cobb, K. L., Risk Factors for Stress Fracture among Young Female Cross-Country Runners. *Medicine & Science in Sports & Exercise* **2007,** 39 (9), 1457-1463.

Appendix A: Daniels' Pace Chart

						Aerobic Threshold		Anaerobic Threshold	
1500m	mile	3000m	2-mile	5000m	10000m	mile	km	mile	km
6:11	6:41	13:11	14:13	22:41	47:04	8:15	5:08	7:42	4:49
6:03	6:32	12:55	13:56	22:15	46:09	8:06	5:02	7:33	4:43
5:56	6:25	12:40	13:40	21:50	45:16	7:57	4:56	7:25	4:38
5:49	6:17	12:26	13:25	21:25	44:25	7:48	4:51	7:17	4:33
5:42	6:10	12:12	13:10	21:02	43:36	7:40	4:46	7:10	4:29
5:36	6:03	11:58	12:55	20:39	42:50	7:32	4:41	7:02	4:24
5:30	5:56	11:45	12:41	20:18	42:04	7:24	4:36	6:55	4:20
5:24	5:50	11:33	12:28	19:57	41:21	7:17	4:31	6:51	4:15
5:18	5:44	11:21	12:15	19:36	40:39	7:09	4:27	6:44	4:11
5:13	5:38	11:09	12:02	19:17	39:59	7:02	4:22	6:38	4:07
5:07	5:32	10:58	11:50	18:58	39:20	6:56	4:18	6:32	4:04
5:02	5:27	10:47	11:39	18:40	38:42	6:49	4:14	6:26	4:00
4:57	5:21	10:37	11:28	18:22	38:06	6:43	4:10	6:20	3:56
4:53	5:16	10:27	11:17	18:05	37:31	6:37	4:06	6:15	3:53
4:48	5:11	10:17	11:06	17:49	36:57	6:31	4:03	6:09	3:50
4:44	5:06	10:08	10:56	17:33	36:24	6:25	3:59	6:04	3:48
4:39	5:02	9:58	10:46	17:17	35:52	6:19	3:55	5:59	3:43
4:35	4:57	9:50	10:37	17:03	35:22	6:14	3:52	5:54	3:40
4:31	4:53	9:41	10:27	16:48	34:52	6:09	3:49	5:50	3:37
4:27	4:49	9:33	10:18	16:34	34:23	6:04	3:46	5:45	3:34
4:24	4:45	9:25	10:10	16:20	33:55	5:59	3:43	5:41	3:32
4:20	4:41	9:17	10:01	16:07	33:28	5:54	3:40	5:36	3:29
4:16	4:37	9:09	9:53	15:54	33:01	5:49	3:37	5:32	3:28
4:13	4:33	9:02	9:45	15:42	32:35	5:45	3:34	5:28	3:24
4:10	4:30	8:55	9:37	15:29	32:11	5:40	3:31	5:24	3:2
4:06	4:26	8:48	9:30	15:18	31:46	5:36	3:28	5:20	3:19
4:03	4:23	8:41	9:23	15:06	31:23	5:32	3:26	5:16	3:16
4:00	4:19	8:34	9:16	14:55	31:00	5:28	3:23	5:13	3:14
3:57	4:16	8:28	9:09	14:44	30:38	5:24	3:21	5:09	3:12
3:54	4:13	8:22	9:02	14:33	30:16	5:20	3:19	5:05	3:10
3:52	4:10	8:16	8:55	14:23	29:55	5:16	3:16	5:02	3:08
3:49	4:07	8:10	8:49	14:13	29:34	5:12	3:14	4:59	3:0
3:46	4:04	8:04	8:43	14:03	29:14	5:09	3:12	4:56	3:0
3:44	4:02	7:58	8:37	13:54	28:55	5:05	3:10	4:52	3:0

Adapted, with permission, from J. Daniels, 2005, *Daniels' Running Formula*, 2nd ed. (Champaign, IL: Human Kinetics), 39, 52, 54.

Notes on Daniels' Pace Chart

This chart can be used to predict **approximate** aerobic and anaerobic thresholds based on your <u>current</u> race fitness. Do not make the common mistake of attempting to force yourself into better shape by running your threshold workouts at the fitness level you *wish* you were at—this is counterproductive. Use a reasonable estimate of your current race fitness. Being too conservative is much better than being too aggressive. Daniels' pace chart can also be used to equate or predict race performances across different distances. All race times are assumed to be in ideal conditions on a track, and you are assumed to be a well-trained athlete (i.e. equally prepared for the mile and the 10k). Times run in inclement weather, on the roads, or over hilly terrain will be slower. See pp. 22-24 for more on using a chart to predict your aerobic and anaerobic thresholds. Times for 800m are not included, since they are highly dependent on anaerobic fitness and as such are not always an accurate reflection of your aerobic conditioning.

For an average male runner, a 1600m race is roughly 1.7 seconds shorter than a full mile. For an average female runner, the difference is about 2.0 seconds. Doubling these numbers to 3.4 and 4.0 seconds, respectively, will allow you to convert 3200m times to two-mile times as well.

Appendix B: Race Pace Chart

400m	800m	1000m	1200m	1500m	1600m	One mile
60	2:00	2:30	3:00	3:45	4:00	4:01.4
61	2:02	2:32	3:03	3:48	4:04	4:05.4
62	2:04	2:35	3:06	3:52	4:08	4:09.4
63	2:06	2:37	3:09	3:56	4:12	4:13.5
64	2:08	2:40	3:12	4:00	4:16	4:17.5
65	2:10	2:42	3:15	4:03	4:20	4:21.5
66	2:12	2:45	3:18	4:07	4:24	4:25.5
67	2:14	2:47	3:21	4:11	4:28	4:29.6
68	2:16	2:50	3:24	4:15	4:32	4:33.6
69	2:18	2:52	3:27	4:18	4:36	4:37.6
70	2:20	2:55	3:30	4:22	4:40	4:41.6
71	2:22	2:57	3:33	4:26	4:44	4:45.7
72	2:24	3:00	3:36	4:30	4:48	4:49.7
73	2:26	3:02	3:39	4:33	4:52	4:53.7
74	2:28	3:05	3:42	4:37	4:56	4:57.7
75	2:30	3:07	3:45	4:41	5:00	5:01.8
76	2:32	3:10	3:48	4:45	5:04	5:05.8
77	2:34	3:12	3:51	4:48	5:08	5:09.8
78	2:36	3:15	3:54	4:52	5:12	5:13.8
79	2:38	3:17	3:57	4:56	5:16	5:17.8
80	2:40	3:20	4:00	5:00	5:20	5:21.9
81	2:42	3:22	4:03	5:03	5:24	5:25.9
82	2:44	3:25	4:06	5:07	5:28	5:29.9
83	2:46	3:27	4:09	5:11	5:32	5:33.9
84	2:48	3:30	4:12	5:15	5:36	5:38.0
85	2:50	3:32	4:15	5:18	5:40	5:42.0
86	2:52	3:35	4:18	5:22	5:44	5:46.0
87	2:54	3:37	4:21	5:26	5:48	5:50.0
88	2:56	3:40	4:24	5:30	5:52	5:54.1
89	2:58	3:42	4:27	5:33	5:56	5:58.1
90	3:00	3:45	4:30	5:37	6:00	6:02.1
91	3:02	3:47	4:33	5:41	6:04	6:06.1
92	3:04	3:50	4:36	5:45	6:08	6:10.1
93	3:06	3:52	4:39	5:48	6:12	6:14.2
94	3:08	3:55	4:42	5:52	6:16	6:18.2
95	3:10	3:57	4:45	5:56	6:20	6:22.2
96	3:12	4:00	4:48	6:00	6:24	6:26.2
97	3:14	4:02	4:51	6:03	6:28	6:30.3
98	3:16	4:05	4:54	6:07	6:32	6:34.3
99	3:18	4:07	4:57	6:11	6:36	6:38.3

3000m	3200m	4000m	5000m	6000m	8000m	10,000m
7:30	8:00	10:00	12:30	15:00	20:00	25:00
7:37	8:08	10:10	12:42	15:15	20:20	25:25
7:45	8:16	10:20	12:55	15:30	20:40	25:50
7:52	8:24	10:30	13:07	15:45	21:00	26:15
8:00	8:32	10:40	13:20	16:00	21:20	26:40
8:07	8:40	10:50	13:32	16:15	21:40	27:05
8:15	8:48	11:00	13:45	16:30	22:00	27:30
8:22	8:56	11:10	13:57	16:45	22:20	27:55
8:30	9:04	11:20	14:10	17:00	22:40	28:20
8:37	9:12	11:30	14:22	17:15	23:00	28:45
8:45	9:20	11:40	14:35	17:30	23:20	29:10
8:52	9:28	11:50	14:47	17:45	23:40	29:35
9:00	9:36	12:00	15:00	18:00	24:00	30:00
9:07	9:44	12:10	15:12	18:15	24:20	30:25
9:15	9:52	12:20	15:25	18:30	24:40	30:50
9:22	10:00	12:30	15:37	18:45	25:00	31:15
9:30	10:08	12:40	15:50	19:00	25:20	31:40
9:37	10:16	12:50	16:02	19:15	25:40	32:05
9:45	10:24	13:00	16:15	19:30	26:00	32:30
9:52	10:32	13:10	16:27	19:45	26:20	32:55
10:00	10:40	13:20	16:40	20:00	26:40	33:20
10:07	10:48	13:30	16:52	20:15	27:00	33:45
10:15	10:56	13:40	17:05	20:30	27:20	34:10
10:22	11:04	13:50	17:17	20:45	27:40	34:35
10:30	11:12	14:00	17:30	21:00	28:00	35:00
10:37	11:20	14:10	17:42	21:15	28:20	35:25
10:45	11:28	14:20	17:55	21:30	28:40	35:50
10:52	11:36	14:30	18:07	21:45	29:00	36:15
11:00	11:44	14:40	18:20	22:00	29:20	36:40
11:07	11:52	14:50	18:32	22:15	29:40	37:05
11:15	12:00	15:00	18:45	22:30	30:00	37:30
11:22	12:08	15:10	18:57	22:45	30:20	37:55
11:30	12:16	15:20	19:10	23:00	30:40	38:20
11:37	12:24	15:30	19:22	23:15	31:00	38:45
11:45	12:32	15:40	19:35	23:30	31:20	39:10
11:52	12:40	15:50	19:47	23:45	31:40	39:35
12:00	12:48	16:00	20:00	24:00	32:00	40:00
12:07	12:56	16:10	20:12	24:15	32:20	40:25
12:15	13:04	16:20	20:25	24:30	32:40	40:50
12:22	13:12	16:30	20:37	24:45	33:00	41:15

Appendix C: Sample Workout Schedules

Here are some examples of how you can incorporate the various elements discussed in this book into a training program. Please note that these schedules are only <u>examples</u> intended to illustrate how to put together a comprehensive plan; they are not a standalone program! The particulars of proper training (including workouts, mileage, and so on) will depend on your training history, goals, race distance, and fitness level.

Two sample weeks are included for each of the three phases of training: the aerobic development phase, the anaerobic development phase, and the racing phase (or, as my high school coach put it, **base**, **pace**, and **race**). The first schedule is for a younger or less experienced runner—perhaps a high school sophomore or junior with a year or two of running. The second is for an older and more experienced athlete—say, a high school senior or a freshman in college.

Both schedules assume you are preparing for a 5k race; a middle distance runner would emphasize relaxed speedwork and shorter race-pace intervals earlier and more often. Your primary race distance has a greater effect on your workout schedule as your season progresses; a miler and a 5k or 10k runner can do very similar training during the base phase, but will begin to diverge as race-specific workouts begin in the pace phase. See p. 79 for a sample workout schedule for middle-distance runners.

Ancillary training like plyometrics and strength work are not included, but should be done 2-3 times per week. All workouts should be preceded by a 10-15min warm-up jog plus some sprint drills and strides, and should be followed by a 10-15min cool-down jog.

Base Phase (summer for a cross country runner)

<u>Younger runner—Total: ~ 40-50 miles</u>
Mon   45min at moderate effort (not easy, but not
         hard either)
Tue   50min easy
Wed   60min easy
Thu   45min easy + sprint drills and 5x100m strides
Fri   5mi progression run (see p. 21)
Sat   80min long run at easy pace
Sun   Off *or* 25-30min very easy

<u>Older runner—Total: ~ 70-80 miles</u>
Mon   7mi AT run (see p. 20) *or* 8x3min at AnT w/ 60sec
         jog recovery (see p. 21)
Tue   AM: 60min easy PM: 30min easy + sprint drills
         and 5x100m strides
Wed   80-90min easy
Thu   AM: 60min easy PM: 30min easy + sprint drills
         and 4x150m strides
Fri   7mi progression run
Sat   100-105min long run at easy pace
Sun   35-45min very easy

Comments

While both schedules focus on aerobic development, a more experienced runner can to take on a more complex schedule that incorporates a larger proportion of targeted high-end aerobic work (the AT run/cruise intervals), more sessions to target running economy (drills and strides), and more volume overall. Whether you are a younger or older runner, you must take care not to push the pace on Monday and Friday—the intent of these workouts is to practice running *fast*, not *hard*!

You should ramp up your mileage gradually during the base phase, starting with only easy running and perhaps some strides, then build your volume by 10% or so each week. Once you are close to your goal mileage, you can add in high-end aerobic workouts like the ones above.

Pace phase (early to mid-fall for a cross country runner)

Younger runner—Total: ~ 40-50 miles
Mon	20min AnT run
Tue	45-50min easy
Wed	Race pace workout: 6-7x800m at 5k pace with 3min jog recovery *or* hill workout, etc.
Thu	50min easy
Fri	40-45min easy + sprint drills and 5x100m strides
Sat	RACE or 70-80min long run at easy pace
Sun	Off *or* 30min very easy

Older runner—Total: ~ 60-70 miles
Mon	5x1500m at AnT with 60sec jog recovery
Tue	AM: 60min easy PM: 30min easy + sprint drills and 5x100m strides
Wed	Race pace workout: 5x1200m at 5k pace with 3min jog recovery *or* hill workout, etc.
Thu	AM: 60min easy PM: 30min easy
Fri	40-60min easy *or* 20-30min easy + sprint drills and two sets of 5x150m strides *or* 16x200m at 3k-1mi pace with 200m jog recovery
Sat	RACE *or* 90min long run at easy pace
Sun	30-50min very easy

Comments

During the pace phase, your volume should not drop precipitously. There are benefits for each type of anaerobic threshold workout; AnT runs are useful for practicing continuous running at a steady pace, while cruise interval workouts allow you to do a larger overall volume of threshold running. Both younger and older runners should practice each type of AnT workout (cruise intervals and continuous AnT runs) at some point, though runners of all abilities are more prone to "cheat" cruise interval sessions by running the repeats too fast, defeating the purpose of the workout. Older runners can handle longer repeats and more total volume, both in Monday's cruise interval session and the 5k pace workout on Wednesday. Even midway into the season, it is prudent to include one high-end aerobic workout (progression run, AT run, AnT run, or cruise intervals) every week so you don't lose sight of aerobic development, the main determiner of long-term success.

On this schedule, Wednesdays are "staple session" workouts, which are usually race-specific intervals, hill workouts, or other high-intensity work. These workouts can double as a VO_2 max session if you're doing 3k-5k pace. Even if you are a college runner preparing for longer races, you ought to do at least some sustained running at 3k-5k pace or faster every few weeks. Finally, if you are a more experienced runner, you can incorporate more focused "mechanical" training sessions (Friday) once every two weeks or so to improve efficiency and speed. Younger runners are better served by getting in more aerobic mileage.

Race phase (late fall for a cross country runner)

Younger runner—Total: ~ 30-40 miles
Mon 4x1000m at 5k pace with 3min jog recovery
Tue 35-45min easy
Wed 25min AT run *or* 6x3min at AnT with 60sec
     jog recovery
Thu 30-45min easy
Fri 20-30min easy + sprint drills and 4x100m strides
Sat MAJOR RACE
Sun Off *or* 20-30min very easy

<u>Older runner—Total: ~ 45-60 miles</u>

Mon 5x1000m at 5k pace with 3min jog recovery
Tue AM: 20-30min easy (*optional*)
     PM: 50-60min easy + sprint drills and 5x100m strides
Wed 7-8x3min at AnT with 60sec jog recovery
     or 30min AT run
Thu AM: 20-30min easy (*optional*)
     PM: 45-60min easy
Fri 30-35min easy + sprint drills and 4x100 strides
Sat MAJOR RACE
Sun 35min very easy

Comments

Generally I don't think it is wise to suddenly cut your mileage or introduce new types of workouts immediately prior to a big race (though see pp. 57-58 for the range of opinions on peaking). In this schedule, you reduce your volume only a bit and switch your focus to practicing *how* to race. For both younger and older runners, this means a race-pace workout that is not very difficult on Monday so you can practice running the appropriate pace. The repeats are also long enough to discourage running them too fast—a common problem when your last major workout includes fast 200s or 400s.

The short Wednesday AT run reinforces your ability to maintain an even pace for a race-like duration without inducing acidosis during the workout. Another option is an anaerobic threshold workout on Wednesday as a "return to basics" effort that won't throw anything off-kilter three days out from a race. The rest of the runs are just long enough to maintain your current fitness.

Modifications for a Middle Distance Runner

True middle distance specialists—those with swift speed over 400m and better performance over 800m than 3000m or two miles—should recognize that their strongest assets are their speed and stamina. As such, they should not neglect faster running, even during the base phase. It is still necessary to stimulate the aerobic system to foster long-term development, but without straying too far from faster paces.

The way to do this is with fast but relaxed interval sessions that touch on race-relevant speeds without incurring the large oxygen debts of classic middle-distance workouts; these can come later in the training cycle, if needed. As with the previous schedules, if you are an older, more experienced runner, you can add in doubles and more workout volume, while novices can pare down the volume and intensity.

Base phase (winter for a track runner)

Middle Distance Runner—Total: ~ 35-65 miles

Mon   6-8x3min at AnT w/ 60sec jog recovery *or* 20min AnT run *or* 30-35min AT run *or* 10-12x300m at 5k pace w/ 100 jog recovery

Tue   35-60min easy + sprint drills and 6x100m strides

Wed   12-16x200m at 3k to mile pace w/ 200m jog recovery *or* 50min fartlek run with 10x1min fast/2min easy *or* 40-60min unstructured fartlek run over hills

Thu   35-60min easy

Fri   20min easy + sprint drills + 2-3 sets of 5x100m strides with 8-10min walk/jog between sets *or* 35-60min easy + sprint drills and 6x100m strides

Sat   60-90min long run over hills at easy pace *or* 35-60min easy

Sun   Off *or* 30min very easy

Comments

As a middle distance runner, you can take a more balanced approach to training during the base phase, setting aside time each week to train speed, stamina, high-end aerobic endurance, and volume. The mileage range is wider, considering that individual middle distance runners respond to long aerobic running to differing extents. The variety of the Wednesday workouts allows for variation in both speed and training venue—a high quality track is often not available in the winter, but at the same time, the monotony of track workouts can be mentally exhausting, even if the physical work is not.

As a replacement, you can do a fartlek workout: a regular easy run with bursts of faster running interspersed. These bursts of speed can be planned beforehand (e.g. a 50min run with 10x1min fast/2min easy) or, in a "true" or "unstructured" fartlek workout, can be done completely by feel—running fast until you get tired, then running easy until you feel good again. Fartlek workouts have the benefits of being more aerobic and less strenuous than a traditional interval workout on the track.

As technique is particularly important for middle distance races, you can dedicate one day every week or two (Friday on this schedule) solely to improving mechanics with 2-3 sets of strides with plenty of recovery. Lastly, Saturday's weekly or biweekly long run ensures that pure endurance is not a lingering weakness that will impair your performance down the road.

Pace phase (early spring for a track runner)

Middle Distance Runner—Total: ~ 35-60miles

Mon   8x150m at 400m pace with 3min recovery
or 16x200m descending from 3k pace to 800m pace
with 200m walk/jog recovery
or 4-5x800m at 3k pace with 3min recovery

Tue   35-60min easy + sprint drills and 4x150m strides

Wed   8x300m at 800m pace with 2min recovery
or 3x500m at 800m pace with 8-10min recovery
or 6x500m at mile pace with 2.5-3min recovery
or other "staple" race pace workout

Thu   35-60min easy

Fri   30-45min easy + sprint drills and 4x100 strides

Sat   RACE *or* 60-80min long run over hills at easy pace
or 8x3min at AnT w/ 60sec jog recovery *or* 20min
AnT run *or* 30-35min AT run

Sun   Off *or* 20-35min very easy

Comments

For a middle distance runner, the anaerobic development or "pace" phase allows for greater variety in workouts.
Your emphasis should still be balanced among speed, endurance, and stamina, but as the racing season approaches, your
race-specific workouts (Wednesday) should take precedence
over speed and endurance workouts (Monday). There is still
room for high end aerobic workouts and long runs, but only in
weeks without a race.

With respect to specific workouts, there are several
options which are largely dictated by whether you are preparing primarily for the 800m or the mile and 1500m. As usual, it
is important not to run your workouts *aggressively*, since this
will be counter-productive to developing fitness. The "staple"
workouts on Wednesday are strenuous but not so difficult as
to exceed your ability to recover within a few days. Ideally,

the day after a difficult anaerobic workout or a race should involve some easy jogging instead of total rest to flush out any metabolic byproducts from the muscles.

Race phase (late spring for a track runner)

<u>Middle Distance Runner—Total: ~ 30-50mi</u>

Mon   10x100m accelerating from one mile pace to 400m pace, easy 100m walk/jog between *or* 8x200m at 800m pace with 200m jog recovery

Tue   30-60min easy

Wed   8x200m at 800m race pace with 2min recovery *or* 10-12x200m at mile pace with 2min recovery

Thu   25-60min easy

Fri   20-30min easy + sprint drills and 4x100 strides

Sat   MAJOR RACE

Sun   20-30min very easy

Comments

Much like the race phase for long distance runners, I don't think it is wise to introduce radical changes right before your big races. The same basic structure remains—Monday touching on speed and Wednesday touching on race-specific paces—but the intensity of the workouts is reduced so you are well-rested for race day. At this stage in training, short race-pace repeats are preferable to longer repeats at mile or 800m pace, since these can be quite fatiguing, even when done at the proper pace. Patience is warranted in the racing phase, as it is very easy to use too much energy in the final "tune up" workouts, leaving you drained on race day. Establishing good aerobic fitness in the base and pace phases is essential, since there is little time for high end aerobic work at the end of the middle distance runner's season.

Appendix Summary

The overall principles of training—starting with a base of high volume and high-quality aerobic running, then progressing to race-specific interval workouts and, finally, preparing for your most important races—apply to everyone, regardless of experience or event of choice. However, the specifics, including mileage and individual workouts, are highly variable depending on the runner in question. You should use the sample schedules in this appendix as a guide to *structuring* training, not just as a source for specific workouts. The ideal training schedule is one which strikes the right balance between aerobic training, race-specific speed, endurance, and stamina, and ancillary components like drills and strength work throughout the training cycle.

Appendix D: Glossary of Terms

Below you will find definitions of all of the important terms used in this book. Do note that you may come across other training literature which uses different terminology—since there's no agreement on universal terms for the various paces, phases, and components of training and racing, most coaches invent their own terminology or adapt an amalgam of terms used by others. When communicating about training philosophies, it is very important to be specific. One person's "aerobic power" might be another's "specific endurance" or "critical velocity." Beware of ambiguous terminology!

Acid - Another word for **protons**.

Acidosis - When protons (H^+) released from the breakdown of ATP accumulate in the blood and muscles, causing fatigue.

Aerobic development phase - See **base phase**.

Aerobic drift - A phenomenon where younger or less experienced runners perform much better at shorter distances because their aerobic system is not yet well-trained. As a result, predicting their aerobic or anaerobic thresholds using short-distance PRs will give an overly aggressive estimate of their fitness.

Aerobic respiration - The chemical process used by the **aerobic system**.

Aerobic running - A pace which relies on the aerobic system for the bulk of its energy, meaning that acid does not accumulate, thus avoiding fatigue.

Aerobic system - The process of using oxygen to break pyruvate down into carbon dioxide and water, which regenerates a large amount of ATP and consumes the fatigue-causing protons released when ATP is broken down. Can only take place inside of mitochondria.

Aerobic threshold (AT) - The fastest sustainable pace which does not result in the buildup of acid in the blood and muscles. "Fast but not hard."

Amenorrhea - A lack of menstruation in female runners which is most often caused by disordered eating and is part of the female athlete triad, a serious health issue.

Anaerobic development phase - A 4-8 week period following the base phase where you focus on race-specific fitness through interval workouts and low-key races.

Anaerobic respiration - The chemical process used by the **anaerobic system**.

Anaerobic running - A pace which exceeds the aerobic system's capabilities and results in acid buildup in the blood and muscles.

Anaerobic system - The process of breaking glucose down into pyruvate to regenerate ATP. If pyruvate accumulates, it is converted to lactate.

Anaerobic threshold (AnT) - The fastest pace at which the buildup of acid remains slow and manageable. "Fast, flying" feeling. Roughly equivalent to the pace you could sustain in an all-out race lasting 50-60 minutes.

AnT run - Anaerobic threshold run; a sustained 15-25min run at the anaerobic threshold. Helps improve aerobic fitness.

Arthur Lydiard - A famous coach from New Zealand whose aerobically-oriented training philosophy, developed in the '50s and '60s, revolutionized how distance runners train.

AT run - Aerobic threshold run; a sustained run of 30-60 minutes at the aerobic threshold. Helps improve aerobic fitness.

ATP - Adenosine triphosphate, a chemical which is the fuel for all cellular activity, including muscle contraction. During energy production, it is split into adenosine diphosphate (ADP), a proton (H^+) and a phosphate ion (P_i).

Base phase - The first phase of training, consisting of 10-12 weeks or more of high mileage and high-end aerobic workouts to improve the oxygen delivery system, the aerobic and anaerobic thresholds, and overall fitness.

Bill Bowerman - A renowned coach at the University of Oregon in the mid-20th century who popularized the hard-easy philosophy—separating hard workouts with days of easy running to recover.

Burnout - See **overtraining**.

Cadence - See **stride frequency**.

Calcium - A mineral found in dairy products and leafy green vegetables that is essential for maintaining bone health. Competes with iron for absorption.

Capillaries - Very small blood vessels that deliver oxygen and remove waste products from the muscles. Training increases their number and size.

Carbohydrates - Dietary sources of sugars, which are broken down into glucose and used in the muscles for energy during exercise.

Cardiac output - A measurement of the heart's ability to move blood through the blood vessels and deliver oxygen to the muscles.

Cooldown - A routine of 10-20 minutes of easy running and, optionally, light drills and stretching which should follow workouts and races.

Cruise intervals - An interval workout with repeats at the anaerobic threshold which are between 3 and 15 minutes long, separated by short recovery periods.

Dynamics - See **sprint drills**.

Endurance - Your ability to sustain moderate paces slower than the speed of your primary race distance. Developed by high-end aerobic training and interval workouts consisting of long repeats with short recovery periods.

Efficiency - See **running economy**.

Even splits - When your intermediate split times in a race or workout are nearly equivalent.

Fartlek - Swedish for "speed play." A regular easy run with several surges of faster running in the middle, each being anywhere from 30 seconds to over 10 minutes. In a "true" or "unstructured" fartlek, the bursts of fast running and the recovery in between are done entirely by feel.

Fast twitch - A characteristic of a muscle fiber which can contract quickly and use the phosphocreatine and anaerobic energy systems to generate large amounts of power very quickly.

Female athlete triad - A serious health problem characterized by disordered eating, low bone density, and a lack of menstruation that occurs in female runners.

Ferritin - An iron transport protein that circulates in the blood, supplying iron to the body when needed. Low ferritin levels can impair performance.

Form drills - See **sprint drills**.

Free ATP - The supply of ATP in your muscle cells at rest. Only lasts a few seconds.

General strength - Your body's overall muscular strength and athleticism. Important for performance and injury prevention. Improved by doing strength exercises.

Glucose - A simple form of sugar that is the fuel for the aerobic and anaerobic energy systems. Comes from the carbohydrates in your diet.

Glycogen - A long chain of glucose molecules linked together. Used to store glucose in your body.

Glycolysis - The scientific term for the **anaerobic system**.

H^+ - The chemical symbol for **protons**.

Hemoglobin - An iron-containing protein which makes up red blood cells, allowing them to transport oxygen to the muscles. Low hemoglobin levels indicate iron deficiency.

High-end aerobic - Describes workouts which directly stimulate the aerobic and anaerobic thresholds. Includes AT runs, AnT runs, progression runs, and cruise intervals.

Interval workout - A training session which consists of repeated bouts of fast running, either for a specified time or duration (e.g. 6x4min or 8x1000m) with recovery periods of easy jogging and, in high speed workouts with long recovery periods, walking.

Iron - A nutrient found in red meat, legumes, and fortified foods which is essential for maintaining healthy hemoglobin and ferritin levels. Absorption is inhibited by calcium.

Lactate - A byproduct of the anaerobic energy system, which supplies additional ATP when the aerobic system cannot keep pace with the ATP demands during exercise. While lactate itself does not cause fatigue, it correlates well with levels of acidity, so blood lactate levels are used as a proxy for an athlete's level of fatigue.

Lactic acid - A misused term which conflates the roles of lactate—a byproduct of the anaerobic system and a useful marker for proton levels—and protons, the true cause of fatigue. "Acid" and "acidosis" are more appropriate terms to refer to the metabolic fatigue associated with fast paces.

Lactate threshold - Another term for the **anaerobic threshold**.

Long run - A continuous run at an easy or moderate pace that is around 1.5 times as far as a "normal" easy run. For most runners, this means their long run will constitute about 20% of their weekly mileage. Typically, long runs are done on a weekly or biweekly basis.

Marathon pace - Your theoretical maximum speed over a marathon, which corresponds to your **aerobic threshold**.

Maximum steady state - See **aerobic threshold**.

Mitochondria - Special structures inside muscle cells where the aerobic system regenerates ATP. Training causes the number of mitochondria in your muscles to multiply.

Muscle fiber - The basic unit which makes up muscles. They come in a variety of types, which dictate how quickly or efficiently the muscle fiber can generate power.

Negative splits - When your intermediate split times in a workout or race get progressively faster.

Overstriding - Occurs when your stride length is too long for a given pace. Increases impact forces and causes excessive strain on your legs. Boosting your stride frequency is an easy way to keep overstriding in check.

Overtraining - When a lack of recovery and excessive training, particularly hard anaerobic workouts and races, overwhelm the body and causes excessive fatigue, poor performance, and possibly injuries.

Oxygen debt - The resultant fatigue due to acidosis which occurs when running at speeds faster than the aerobic threshold. The "debt" itself is the amount of energy required for a given pace in excess of what can be produced by the aerobic system.

Oxygen delivery system - The combination of the heart, lungs, blood vessels, and blood cells which deliver oxygen from the air in your lungs to your muscles, where it is used by the aerobic system.

Pace phase - Another term for the **anaerobic development phase**.

Peaking - The alterations (if any) you make in training volume and workout intensity at the end of your competitive season as the most important races approach.

Phosphocreatine system - The first energy system used to regenerate ATP during a high-intensity effort. The chemical phosphocreatine splits into phosphate and creatine, donating the phosphate to spent ADP. Lasts for around eight seconds during an all-out effort.

Plyometrics - Explosive, dynamic, and high-impact exercises which stimulate the fast-twitch muscle fibers, improving speed and efficiency.

Positive splits - When your intermediate split times in a workout or race get progressively slower.

Progression run - A high-end aerobic workout that stimulates both the aerobic and anaerobic thresholds. The run starts off extremely easy, but over the course of several miles, gradually accelerates to a pace around the aerobic threshold. In the final mile or two, the pace can accelerate to the anaerobic threshold or faster, though the workout should end *before* you feel the effects of acidosis.

Protein - The main nutrient your body uses to rebuild your muscles after a workout. Good sources include lean meats, dairy, eggs, and beans. Can boost recovery when consumed along with carbohydrates within 15 minutes of a workout.

Protons - A byproduct of ATP breakdown. When they accumulate in the muscles or in the blood, acidity increases. Denoted by the chemical symbol H^+.

Pyruvate - The product of the first step of the anaerobic system, which breaks down glucose. Used by the aerobic system to produce additional energy. When the aerobic system is at its limit, pyruvate accumulates and is turned into lactate to delay acid buildup.

Race (or racing) phase - The final period in a training cycle, when the focus becomes being well-prepared and well-recovered for the most important races of the season. Your peak racing shape can be maintained for 4-6 weeks before your aerobic conditioning begins to deteriorate.

Racing flats - Thin, lightweight running shoes which can be worn during workouts to increase speed, achieve greater calf and ankle range of motion, and mimic racing conditions.

Running economy - A measurement of how efficiently your body turns the oxygen it consumes into forward motion. Can be improved by strides, drills, plyometrics, strength training, high mileage, and high-end aerobic workouts.

Slow twitch - A characteristic of a muscle fiber which can use the aerobic system to efficiently generate muscular force for a long time without allowing fatigue to accumulate.

Speed - Your ability to run at paces significantly faster than the speed of your primary race. Developed by interval workouts with short repeats and long recovery periods.

Sprint drills - Dynamic drills and exercises designed to improve coordination, emphasize certain aspects of the running stride, and enhance joint range of motion.

Stamina - Your ability to sustain a fast pace—usually the speed of your primary race distance—for a long time. Developed by interval workouts with medium-length repeats and moderate recovery periods.

Stride frequency - The rate at which your feet hit the ground. Typically denoted in strides per minute. Higher stride frequencies reduce the stress on your legs for a given pace.

Strides - Short, relaxed, fast repeats of 100-200m (15-35 seconds) with at least an equal jog recovery in between designed to improve speed and running economy. Can be done after easy runs and before workouts and races.

Tempo run - An ambiguous term which usually refers to a fast, continuous run at either the AT or AnT. When discussing tempo runs it is important to specify the pace and distance.

Training cycle - A roughly six-month block of training dedicated to preparing for a specific racing season which falls at the end of the cycle.

Vitamin C - A nutrient found in citrus fruits and leafy green vegetables which boosts iron absorption.

Vitamin D - A nutrient found in fish and fortified foods which boosts calcium absorption. Can also be synthesized inside your body by exposure to direct sunlight.

VO$_2$ max - The slowest pace which elicits your maximum heart rate and maximum oxygen consumption. Falls between 3k and 5k race pace.

Warmup - A combination of 10-20 minutes of easy running, sprint drills, and several strides which should precede all of your workouts and races.

About the Author

John Davis is a runner, writer, and student of the sport. He competed for Eden Prairie High School (Minnesota) and Carleton College, where he studied chemistry. John now lives and works in the Minneapolis/St. Paul metropolitan area, performing research, speaking, and writing about training, racing, and running injuries while coaching at a local high school. His blog, Running Writings, provides detailed analysis of coaching philosophies, summaries of scientifically-vetted ways to treat and prevent injury, and insights into training and racing. His first booklet, <u>Basic Training Principles for Middle and Long-Distance Running</u>, is available for free at Running-Writings.com. He can be reached via email at john@runningwritings.com.

Acknowledgements

I am grateful for the help of friends and family who reviewed, commented on, and criticized the various drafts of this book and provided support along the way. I am also deeply indebted to Jack Daniels, Laura Roach, Greg Rhodes, Kenny Moore, and Bruce Mortenson for their assistance gathering and preparing the necessary pictures, graphs, and data for this book. Finally, I'd like to thank you, the reader! Your support makes all the hard work worth it.

CPSIA information can be obtained
at www.ICGtesting.com
Printed in the USA
LVHW051340201218
601203LV00014B/1207/P